SLA | GUIDELINES plus

Plans, Practices and Policies

Information Literacy and the Secondary School Library

Geoff Dubber

Series Editor: Geoff Dubber

School Library Association

Acknowledgements

I would like to give special thanks to the following colleagues and friends who have all contributed to this publication – Lynne Varley, Chris Shercliff, Nicola Mason and Liz Smith who provided really useful case studies or information, Claire Larson and Annike Dase who read and commented on the text for me and Richard Leveridge and Jane Cooper in the SLA office who turn draft manuscripts into real publications for us! Thanks too to everyone who attends my ILS sessions and provides me with such a wealth of ideas and of course to colleagues on the joint SLG/SLA IL Task Force and to SLN members far and wide who endlessly discuss all aspects of ILS and its related research.

Published by

School Library Association
1 Pine Court, Kembrey Park
Swindon
SN2 8AD

Tel: 01793 530166 Fax: 01793 481182
Email: info@sla.org.uk
Web: www.sla.org.uk

Registered Charity No: 313660
Charity Registered in Scotland No: SC039453

Printed by Rumbold Holland Litho Ltd, Swindon

Contents

66 The creation of an Information Society is key to social, cultural and economic development of nations and communities, institutions and individuals in the 21st century and beyond.

Information Literacy should be an integral part of Education for all, which can contribute critically to the achievement of the United Nations Millennium Development Goals, and respect for the Universal Declaration 99 of Human Rights.

—*The Prague Declaration*

66 The idea of a librarian as an academic expert who is available to talk about assignments and hold their hands through the research process is... foreign to most students. 99

—'What Students Don't Know'. 22 Aug. 2011. *Inside Higher Ed.* http://goo.gl/oe7Jd Accessed 22 December 2011

66 School librarians have... power – we are the loom to help pupils weave information into the fabric of knowledge. 99

—Sally Dring. *The School Librarian*. Autumn 2011, p.136

Note: For the purposes of this publication, Information Literacy (IL) and Information Literacy Skills (ILS) are synonymous.

Never before in the history of the planet have so many people – on their own – had the ability to find so much information about so many things and about so many people.[1]

In the seven years since the last SLA guideline on Information Literacy Skills (ILS) for secondary school library staff was published, there have been marked changes to the secondary school curriculum with greater emphasis on skills and information literacy. Huge investment has been made in ICT provision for schools, sometimes to the detriment of the library. Social networking has gained immense popularity and importance in our lives. In the world beyond school most of us have experienced the economic downturn – the full effects are perhaps only now being felt in schools and school libraries. These changes and the altered educational and economic climate in which we work have meant that the role and work of school libraries have come under scrutiny as never before and the need for school library staff to deliver more directed, coherent, progressive and curriculum based information skills programmes has never been greater, or indeed more important.

Recent changes

To put the changing information literacy scene into perspective, consider how the following have affected your own library management practices and policies over the last half decade…

- New curricula have arrived for the secondary phase in each of the home countries and in the Republic of Ireland, (more is expected in England with further changes to the National Curriculum) that give greater emphasis to skills work, thinking, problem solving and independent learning – what do you know about them?

- New exams now offer increased weighting to project work with an emphasis on independent research and learning – e.g. the Extended Project Qualification, Diplomas and the increasingly popular International Baccalaureate. Which exams are used in your school and how do they impact on the library?

- Web 2.0 has emerged as a real tool for creating and sharing information in ways never considered even a few years ago – how do you use it to promote Information Literacy?

- Wikipedia and You Tube are now common place first stop information sources for all students in secondary schools – what's your attitude?

- Google has become ever more important – most students use precious few other search engines thinking that Google is sufficient to point them to the sites that they need. How do you counter that or do you work with it?

---

[1] Friedman, Thomas. *The World is Flat*. Quoted in Godwin. P, and Parker J., *Information Literacy meets Library 2.0*, 2008, Facet Publishing p4.

- Use of non-fiction books in most school libraries has reduced and some librarians are having to consider the percentage of their budget and shelf space devoted to these resources. Are you having problems here and what solutions are you devising?

- OFSTED reported in 2006 on the low level of information skills teaching and learning in a selected sample of England's schools. The situation today appears to show little change – is this an issue for you and how does your library measure up?

- We had these fascinating and useful studies – *Information Behaviour of the Researcher of the Future* from The British Library/JISC looking at the way that the Google generation are searching for and using information and more recently *Truth, Lies & the Internet* from DEMOS.[2]

What do you think?

Is this list already long enough for you? – Draw breath and if you are a super librarian, do have a look at the remainder, if not then skip to the next section

- Electronic whiteboards (IWBs) are now common place in most schools and their potential for demonstrating Internet use and practice is enormous. Can you access one in your library?

- Mobile learning is now also common place in many secondary schools – laptops/tablets, iPads, e-readers and the like, and less commonly mobile phones, are now being used as information sources and processors. What technology is used in your LRC?

- Most secondary schools have a Virtual Learning Environment (VLE) where information can be stored, presented and accessed by the school community. Some school librarians manage their school's VLE and the library has a worthwhile presence – what about yours?

- There has been an increased and sustained interest in the importance of transition/induction strategies for school libraries, not only from the primary phase to the secondary but also from Sixth Form into Higher Education. What strategies do you use?

- School library staff are becoming more aware of the potential for e-learning for developing and reinforcing information literacy, particularly at Sixth Form level. Some are seeing the possibilities of using the excellent H. E. library induction and information skills websites developed by university and other Higher Education librarians. Have you had time to consider the possibilities?

- Many school librarians are now involved in the Extended Schools programmes and enjoy the opportunities this work provides for some in depth information skills work and development with individuals or small groups in the library before or after the school day. Are you involved?

[2] http://www.jisc.ac.uk/media/documents/programmes/reppres/
   gg_final_keynote_11012008.pdf

   http://www.demos.co.uk/publications/truth-lies-and-the-internet

The information literacy world is changing fast. This guideline will address the main issues facing school librarians as they support students and adult colleagues in the second decade of the 21st century to find and use information.

It will cover key areas such as:

- Providing a clear definition/explanation of information literacy skills
- Terminology – what do we call these vitally important skills and sub-skills?
- The importance of working in a known and agreed curriculum context in partnership with teaching colleagues – going it alone really isn't viable or credible. Talking curriculum is essential
- Library management issues and strategies that will impinge on Information Literacy and its delivery
- Strategies for working with teachers
- Looking at areas that are new to many people – progression, assessment and evaluation
- Putting together an Information Skills policy/strategy for the library and of course working with all age ranges – although time is usually in short supply it is important to work across the age range and not focus simply on the 11 or the 16-year-olds.

Chapter One

Helping to prepare our students for their information world

Consider the information world of our students in school according to *The Economist*:[3]

- Wal-Mart handles more than 1 million customer transactions every hour

- Decoding the human genome took 10 years when first finished in 2003, it can now be done in one week!

- The amount of digital information increases 10 times every 5 years! Google has over 2.7 billion searches per month

- The amount of reading people do has almost tripled since 1980 – thanks to the internet

- Bristol University's BlueCrystal 2 was one of the fastest computers in the UK when it was installed a year ago. It can do 37 trillion computations a second[4]

- In May 2011 some 36,660,000 unique web visitors logged on in Britain. They spent an average of 33.9 hours reading or working on line, and visited an average of 3,079 webpages.[5]

If that is mind blowing, then have a look at the following clips on You Tube:

Shift Happens: Bringing Education Into The 21st Century
http://www.youtube.com/watch?v=lg27w_Ylx0sand

Learning Potential Our Future
http://www.youtube.com/watch?v=b7RPfsxFUYgandfeature=fvw

How are we in the school library world helping to prepare our children for *their* information world?

Do you recognize these situations?

- Perhaps you're new to your school and feel this could be your main focus of work.

- Perhaps you've spent a good deal of time on reader development and now want to redirect your efforts?

---

[3] *The Economist*. 'Data Data Everywhere'. 27 Feb. 2010
[4] *The Observer*. 21 March 2010
[5] Quoted in *The Observer* (date unknown) with data obtained from http://www.comscore.com/

- Perhaps you feel at a distance from your teaching colleagues, you feel frustrated that your senior leadership team and the teachers in general don't appear to understand your potential to support the curriculum?

- Perhaps you want to be seen for what you are – the library professional and knowledge manager?

- Perhaps the students think that you sit and read books all day and know little about their learning or perhaps there is a multitude of information handling going on in your library on a daily basis as students and possibly teachers use the PCs/laptops and Internet and you know little about its context. You also feel that some of the practice you see is less than satisfactory.

- Perhaps you feel a little jaded sometimes.

Been there! Done that! I have been here eight years now and although I raise the profile of the library, have a good stock, basically tick all the right boxes, the departments still aren't making good use of the library. [6]

Start at the Beginning

If you're keen to make a difference with information literacy and help your students cope confidently and effectively with the amazing world of information out there, then start at the beginning.

Consider the official line, represented by OFSTED's *Good School Libraries* paper in 2006: [7]

- The quality of many of the IL sessions seen were poor. The sessions were often superficial, repeated what the pupils already knew and did not form part of a coherent programme. Provision was often not consolidated through learning across the curriculum.

- The survey found many weaknesses overall in pupils' understanding and use of information and research skills (the OFSTED team also saw some excellent practice).

- Lessons in 'library skills' were often unsatisfactory and not underpinned sufficiently by whole-school agreement on what was to be taught at each stage. In general, there were too few opportunities for pupils to carry out a search or work independently to prepare them for further education or the workplace.

- Schools acknowledged they were not successful enough in involving subjects across the curriculum in information literacy. Senior managers

---

[6] Quote from a colleague of mine on the SLA Board!

[7] OFSTED *Good School Libraries: Making a Difference to Learning*, March 2006. Ref. HMI2624.

were not sufficiently active in managing this work. Librarians who lacked this support found it difficult to involve reluctant departments.

There is no clear evidence to prove that the national picture has improved, although of course there are pockets of excellent practice to be found in all sectors and all parts of the UK and Great Britain.

What do you think?

14 questions that might help to shape your initial thinking

1. What's your understanding/expertise with information literacy? When did you last read anything about its theories and practices or attend INSET on the subject?

2. What do you know about the information handling practices of the so called Google generation and how do you currently support your students?

3. Does the school or the library have an information skills policy framework? In reality how do your students learn to effectively handle information – trial and error? osmosis? mish-mash from departments or planned progression?

4. Does the school understand your present contribution and work effort do you assess and measure any of your ILS contributions or is it mostly guess work?

5. How much time have you available to focus on information literacy? Are you a one person band in a large school with time only to do the immediate? Can you give time to this vital initiative? What might you give up in order to do more for ILS? Is it a strategic priority for you?

6. What real knowledge do you have about the school's curriculum – Year 7 through to the Sixth Form? After all a library can't support a curriculum and an exam system about which it knows little.

7. Do you organise any induction/transition work with any of your years and how much of that overlaps with what could be termed information literacy development?

8. What are your relationships with members of the senior leadership team, teachers, learning assistants etc.? What do they think the library/LRC is for? Do they understand your role and do they understand and use your potential for helping to raise achievement across the school?

9. What does your library/LRC look like? Is it conducive to learning, rather than only fit for teaching?

10. Are all your workstations tucked into one corner or section? Is the library almost another ICT suite used by a constant stream of teachers?

10. What are your day to day library management systems/routines like? Is there room for ILS or are you besieged by groups of Sixth Formers with nowhere else to go, or by pupils sent from other lessons – perhaps simply to use the library ICT without reference to you or to serious use of research skills/techniques?

12. What's your level of confidence? Are you assertive? What does your body language say about you?

13. What have you achieved on the IL front in the previous twelve months?

14. What's your ILS vision for one year and three years hence? How would you really like to make a difference to the independent learning skills and styles of your users – both adults and students?

Being effectively involved with information literacy, the school's curriculum and making changes demands confidence, communication and negotiating skills. You will need a calm and visionary approach – keeping your eye on the horizon rather than on daily details and fighting your corner on occasions, passionately waving that library flag!

What do your answers tell you?

Jot down your thoughts to help your own planning.

Can you discuss any of your observations and general thoughts about ILS progress with your line manager or a member of the senior leadership team? if you feel you can, then start with an informal conversation. However if you can't or don't want to go down that route, then start with your School Library Service/SLS or with members of your SLA branch or contact the SLA office team direct and ask for help. They will probably find you a mentor to share discussion and ideas. You are always very welcome to contact me.

What's your attitude to learning?

It's not something we do to people – they need to do it for themselves.

Consider

Did you enjoy learning at school?

Do you enjoy learning now?

When do you learn best?

Are you aware of the various/different types of learners?

How did your school library help you to learn?

How can you help your students to learn effectively and enjoyably?

How would a sample of your student and staff users answer these questions?

We learn to build new knowledge from existing experiences and understanding – therefore explicitly reflecting on prior knowledge and learning habits is important.

Consider the importance of affective factors (your confidence and feelings towards the subject, the environment and to the teacher/librarian).

Attitude

Think about your own attitude to learning and reflect on

- *one positive learning experience*
- *one experience that was less enjoyable*

Take a look at the excellent Open University Learning How to Learn material at http://openlearn.open.ac.uk/course/view.php?id=1556 This six-hour introductory level course has much to interest everyone

The feelings and confidence levels of the learner are important – a very good reason for the library to be relaxed and welcoming but with a level of structure and guidance.

We want students to naturally apply what they learn in one area to all other areas of the curriculum and the world beyond school.[8]

---

[8] To reflect on learning in more depth take a look at Chapter 1 of James Herring book *Improving Students' Web Use and Information Literacy* (2011, Facet Publishing).

What's your attitude to using information books and the Internet?

Consider the following 'Five Myths About the Information Age':

1. The book is dead

2. We have entered the information age

3. All information is now available online

4. Libraries are obsolete

5. The future is digital

and the answers provided in this interesting article by Robert Darnton at http://chronicle.com/article/5-Myths-About-the-Information/127105/

Start some careful planning...

Consider the following five essential building blocks for IL successfully across the school:

1. Identify your skills – be confident with IL, its skills, its theories and developments and decide its parameters and overlaps with other subjects, especially ICT. You are a key point of authority on IL.

2. Find out what you can about the ILS work and the library experiences of your new intake students from your major primary partner schools.

3. Base all IL work in/on the curriculum.

4. Work in partnership with teaching/support staff colleagues to deliver the curriculum objectives – it's useful if every piece of work you do can be related back and justified in the curriculum.

5. Strengthen your library management structure – links with middle and senior managers so that you can easily join discussions about curriculum development, examination changes and the teaching staff and students see you as knowledgeable and an equal in status in these discussions.

Where are your first priorities here?

Jot down your thoughts

Chapter Two

Information Literacy Skills – some basics

Information literacy should be transformational for the learner, changing their attitude, behaviour, outlook and even their world-view.[9]

We need to walk with kids on the information journey to knowledge… we must intervene instructionally along that journey.[10]

We all talk about these skills, we all accept they are a 'good thing' but what can you do first?

It is important to possess a view of the range and scope of these nebulous skills and their sub-sets. Gone are the days (I hope) when people called them as 'library skills' and they were seen as only to be taught by the librarian in 'library lessons'. They are much more than that – look at the definition lower down this page – and they need to be taught across all curriculum areas, not simply by school library staff. They are part and parcel of every subject as we'll see later on. Unfortunately few in government or the civil servants of any the four home countries call them information literacy skills; teachers seldom do either. Students and parents can be confused by them and the terminology, so we in the school library world are left to do the archaeological work – unearth them from the plethora of curriculum documents and then define, identify and display them for all to see and show their importance and of course our expertise in using them.

Typing *Information Literacy Skills* into Google provides 6,600,000 hits (using the search term "Information Literacy Skills" of course reduces the hits – down to 2,780,000) and Amazon currently advertises 1,058 books on the subject with 69 books on the topic added in the previous 12 months.[11]
So clearly there is a good deal of information about these skills out there even if England's current National Curriculum makes no overt mention of them and the forthcoming repackaged curriculum is likely to be no better.

---

[9] Secker and Coonan. 2011 A New Curriculum for Information Literacy. Executive summary p.5 .Arcadia Project.
http://eprints.lse.ac.uk/37681/1/Executive_summary.pdf
Accessed 30 Sept. 2011.
[10] Quote taken from the School Library Association of Victoria website.
Blog notes from a session led by Ross Todd. Accessed 24 August 2011.
[11] Amazon.co.uk. Accessed 22 August 2011

Definitions

How do we define them?

For simplicity and uniformity it is helpful to use the generally accepted CILIP definition:

Information literacy is knowing when and why you need information, where to find it, and how to evaluate, use and communicate it in an ethical manner.[12]

Alternatively you can use

Information Literacy encompasses knowledge of one's information concerns and needs, and the ability to identify, locate, evaluate, organize and effectively create, use and communicate information to address issues or problems at hand; it is a prerequisite for participating effectively in the Information Society, and is part of the basic human right of life long learning.[13]

For one of the latest definitions Sheila Webber defined IL as:

The adaption of appropriate information behavior [sic] to identify, through whatever channel or medium, information well fitted to information needs, leading to wise and ethical use of information in society.[14]

To make this a little less theoretical and more student friendly, I also like the following produced by Christina Doyle[15] that I have modified slightly.

The **information literate person** (in our case, our student user) is one who:

- Recognises the need for information
- Recognises that accurate and complete information is the basis for intelligent decision making
- Formulates questions based on information needs
- Identifies potential sources of information
- Develops successful search strategies
- Accesses sources of information (*digital and text based*[16])
- Evaluates (I prefer the word Appraises) information
- Organises information for practical application

---

[12] http://www.cilip.org.uk/get-involved/advocacy/learning/information-literacy/pages/definition.aspx

[13] Prague Declaration 'TOWARDS AN INFORMATION LITERATE SOCIETY', 2003

[14] http://www.inforum.cz/pdf/2010/webber-sheila-1.pdf Accessed 22 August 2011. Quoted in Solomon. Wilson. Taylor (2012) 100% Information Literacy Success. Wadsworth Cengage Learning. Boston.

[15] Final report to National Forum on Information Literacy, University of Calgary, Information Literacy Group 1998

[16] my amendment

- Integrates new information into an existing body of knowledge
- Uses information in critical thinking and problem-solving
- *Evaluates the working methods – i.e considers the methods and challenges used to work with information to inform practice on the next occasion.*[17]

If you want to consider other definitions then have a look at http://dis.shef.ac.uk/literacy/definitions.htm

Don't get too focused on academic definitions and descriptions. They are after all the skills of learning to learn needed by all student and in fact all of us, as we research topics and information for our daily lives. They are an active part of the majority of classroom activities. It is the development and practice of these skills that can give the library a major role as a research and information centre for the school; putting it centre stage of the learning in any secondary school. If you believe that, then display your definition and something about their importance in your library.

If you believe in them, stand up for them, shout about their importance!

Remember the old maxim... *when the going gets tough, then the tough get going!*

What you and your colleagues in school call these skills can be a challenge. If you all use different terminology you're likely to spread confusion and make little progress!

Suggestion

Avoid the term 'library skills' at all costs as the skills we're talking about are generic skills not simply those that students need to practice once they step through the door labelled 'library'.

> *I don't see that calling (them) anything new will change how students use what they learn there. They either learn how to find info/judge info etc., or they don't... it is more about the content relating to the rest of their lives, rather than the title.*[18]

It isn't so much what the students call these skills, although it implies that those who don't go near the library don't use them, but rather more what teaching colleagues understand about their scope and depth.

Many of the research/finding out activities carried out by our students start in the classroom, make use of the library, perhaps use other sources of information too – and finish in the classroom or as a piece of homework that

---

[17] my amendment
[18] Discussion on the SLN listserv. 6 May 2010.

could be finished anywhere! These skills certainly are not only library based and the skills needed to be successful are not those solely needed by library users. Much information literacy can be developed without a library – hence the danger with the term.

Literacies

What other names to call these skills?

Dr Daniel Churchill, University of Hong Kong, on his slide share presentation[19] suggests that Information Literacy is only one of seven key literacies that we need – namely:

Traditional Literacy – reading/writing/listening

Information Literacy – the ability to identify what information is needed etc

Visual Literacy – the ability to understand and produce visual messages

Critical Literacy – the ability to question/challenge and evaluate the meanings and purposes of texts

Media Literacy – the ability to question, analyse, interpret, evaluate and create media messages

Tool Literacy – the ability to use tools to manage, consume and create information

Digital Literacy – The ability to use digital technology communication tools, or networks to locate, evaluate, use and create information.

Another Slideshare presentation of some years ago from Otis College Los Angeles suggests that the following literacies overlap to form Information Literacy:[20]

- Media Literacy
- Network Literacy
- Computer Literacy
- Traditional Alphabetic Literacy
- Library Instruction
- Cultural Literacy
- Visual Literacy

---

[19] *New Literacy in the Web 2.0 World.* Slide share. Slide 5. Dr D. Churchill, 2008.
[20] http://www.slideshare.net/verzosaf/information-literacy-implications-for-library-practice-presentation

If that is rather complicated then any of these terms might be useful in discussion with your school colleagues:

- Study Skills
- Research Skills
- Personal, Learning and Thinking Skills (PLTS) – see the DfE definition of these skills[21]
- Learning Skills
- Enquiry Skills
- Guided Enquiry – this is a relatively new term, used in the USA
- Learning to Learn Skills
- Or the now rather dated 1980s term, Resource Based Learning.

Which term do you use and why?

Which term is most common in school – if there isn't one, which would be most useful?

[21] http://curriculum.qcda.gov.uk/key-stages-3-and-4/skills/plts/index.aspx

What do you know about the current information world of our students?

The late Dennis Wise, previously Head of Cramlington Learning Village, six years ago wrote an excellent article *Personalised Learning: Personalised Schooling*.[22] Although the technology has moved on a little, it still rings true today:

> *It's 7 am and John wakes up to the sound of his hi-fi playing his favourite track through his Philips Streamium wireless media box which accesses the music stored downstairs on the living room computer. Wiping the sleep from his eyes, John studies his face in his dressing table mirror which, at the press of a button doubles as a computer screen and television. A red laser light marks out the letters of a computer keyboard onto the dressing table surface and infra red sensors work out what John is typing. John uses the computer to turn on the central heating and his shower. Once downstairs he orders the food for his 16th birthday over the internet via the "kitchen shopper" which reads John's scribbled notes from his tablet PC.[23]*

Our students, the so-called Google or Internet Generation, live in a world of digitisation and digital technologies to a much greater extent than some of us born in earlier decades. They expect to work digitally and to receive information at the press of a button. They often expect to use screens not books and many of their teachers and parents reinforce that attitude. Take a look at http://edorigami.wikispaces.com/21st+Century+Learners.

We know as well as they that the world is full of information. Another good example is this one:

> *It took two centuries to fill the shelves of the Library of Congress with more than 57 million manuscripts, 29 million books and periodicals, 12 million photographs and more. Now the world generates an equivalent amount of digital information nearly 100 times each day.[24]*

And students are reasonably proficient in finding volumes of it – having regular 'information binge'. Unfortunately they often lack the essential skills of selecting, sorting, synthesising and then presenting their newly acquired facts as their own new knowledge.

---

[22] http://www.cchsonline.co.uk/school/teachinglearning/personalisedlearning.pdf
[23] Every piece of technology mentioned in paragraph one is available. See article 'House of the Future Today' in *The Daily Telegraph* of Friday 22 April 2005 quoted http://archive.leadermagazine.co.uk/article.php?id=159 Accessed 22 August 2011.
[24] Internet Innovation Alliance. Quoted in *The Observer*, 6 April 2008.

Students set out with a basket and enjoy an information binge, scooping up everything they can find about a state, a province, a foreign country, a famous person, a battle, a scientific issue or some item already conveniently available in containerized forms within some encyclopedia or book devoted to the subject. This kind of school research puts students in the role of **information consumers** *and demands little thought, imagination or skill.*[25]

Getting information from the Internet is like taking a drink from a fire hydrant[26] but they are often less effective at processing.

Students love cut and paste but often bypass the vital skill of synthesis.

Consider the searching habits of young people

1. As outlined in the excellent report *Information Behaviour of Researchers of the Future* (p12).[27] The authors reported that young people:

   ■ Have not had their IL skills sharpened by access to new technology

   ■ Spend too little time in evaluating information for relevance, accuracy or authority

   ■ Have a strong preference for using 'natural language' rather than using effective key words when using search engines

      I see this all the time at school. Students will type into Google statements such as 'why was Winston Churchill famous?' rather than use key words.[28]

   ■ Often have difficulty in assessing the relevance of information (perhaps because they know little about the subject at the start of their enquiry?)

   ■ Frequently print off pages of information without real regard for content

   ■ Do not understand the way in which that libraries are arranged (the Dewey Decimal Classification system) and do not find it naturally intuitive. Many do not find searching for information through books and journals naturally easy either. Most prefer to use digital resources, and they usually start with a Google search or perhaps with Wikipedia. If we as adults aren't careful with our modelling, and with our encouragement, then their researches tend to be only skin deep.

---

[25] Jamie Mackenzie http://fno.org/dec99/rcycle.html accessed 22 August 2011

[26] http://www.allthatinternet.net/blog/2010/02/%E2%80%9Cgetting-information-off-the-internet-is-like-taking-a-drink-from-a-fire-hydrant-%E2%80%9D-mitchell-kapor/

[27] http://www.jisc.ac.uk/media/documents/programmes/reppres/gg_final_keynote_11012008.pdf accessed 22 August 2011

[28] Quote from Claire Larson who read the draft text for me.

2. And also in the report by James Herring of his work in three Australian schools in **School students, information retrieval and transfer**
Findings from the study indicated that a minority of students both valued and would transfer information retrieval skills.[29]
Implications for teachers and librarians in schools include – the need for more attention to be paid to encouraging students to value I.L. skills before they implement them.[30]

3. Again more recently this interesting study of the research habits of U.S. university students at Illinois University makes similar points:
They tended to overuse Google and misuse scholarly databases. They preferred simple database searches to other methods of discovery, but generally exhibited a 'lack of understanding of search logic'.[31]

Interestingly enough the researchers did not place the onus solely on the students:

Librarians and professors are also partially to blame for the gulf that has opened up between students and the library employees who are supposed to help them... Librarians tend to overestimate the research skills of some of their students... Students are not asking for help and knowing what kind of help they need...[32]

To many of us this is also a familiar picture of school student researcher habits here in the UK.

What are your own feelings and what strategies do you use to combat these challenges – are they effective?

What would make them more effective?

So we need a range of plans, practices and policies to develop and promote the necessary skills if we are really going to put the LRC and the librarian centre stage in the school's information environment.

[29] http://www.lirg.org.uk/lir/ojs/index.php/lir/article/viewFile/242/301
Accessed 23 August 2011
[30] ibid. p.15
[31] What Students Don't Know. *Inside Higher Ed.* 22 August 2011
http://www.insidehighered.com/news/2011/08/22/erial_study_of_student_
research_habits_at_illinois_university_libraries_reveals_alarmingly_
poor_information_literacy_and_skills
[32] ibid.

Chapter Three

The Research Cycle

I'm still discussing a whole school framework with my line manager and have been banging on about it for five years or so! I want to tie it in with plagiarism and planning research. Am sick of staff coming in for a research lesson and saying 'your project will be ten pages long, needs to have a cover, a title page and a contents page. Miss will explain where the books are…' and then they wonder why they get back plagiarised/disorganised/generally poor quality work back!

*Would love to do an INSET and give **them** a task with equally vague instructions and see how they get on, just to make the point…[33]*

In our daily lives we are constantly planning a sequence of personal tasks, finding information to suit our needs, managing our time and solving problems – fundamental life skills. These are processes familiar to all. Information seeking and with it turning information into personal knowledge follows a similar process:

- Consider the task/define the problem
- Locate and identify information to suit the purpose
- Assess the worth of the information
- Build new knowledge/make decisions based on the information available
- Communicate the actions/the new knowledge
- Evaluate the process that we took.

This is the fundamental start point for information literacy for any learner – making the process explicit to our library users and discussing the stages is essential – it gives them ownership of their own thought processes. It will give them greater understanding of this innate process, enable them to pinpoint their planning for and location on their specific research journey and hopefully give them a clearer idea of their destination.

---

[33] Email from a friend on the SLA Board: 1 October 2009.

Consider a common find out/fact finding/investigative task of your own:

– perhaps you want to buy a new car

– what is your research sequence?

Imagine that you want to visit Machu Picchu in Peru for your next holiday – you want to learn about the site and decide what clothes would be useful:

What essential skills would you use and in what sequence – with what success?

Searching for the 'right' information is a sophisticated skill.

Make your choice!

Choose your IL research process and consider the skills

Take a look at the wide variety available on http://www.shambles.net/pages/learning/infolit/infolitmod/ or http://virtualinquiry.com/inquiry/models.htm and see also Appendix 1 (p76).

Browse the ones that interest you and then pay special regard to the following five examples that are most popular with UK schools and school library staff:

- The ever popular U.S.Big6™ model of Mike Eisenberg and Bob Berkowitz widely promoted in the United States and Canada

- The PLUS model of James Herring – essentially a basic framework rather than a self help sequence for learners

- The Seven Pillars of Information Literacy widely disseminated through Higher Education, now being reassessed by the Research Information Network (RIN) team[34]

- The Big Blue Connect model that uses eight stages[35]

- The Kuhlthau model – developed and promoted by Carol Kuhlthau as part of her Guided Enquiry work (essentially another name for IL). The value of this process is that it includes not only the steps needed for research by the complementary sequence of Thoughts, Feelings,

[34] See http://www.informationliteracy.org.uk/ Accessed 23 August 2011.
[35] See http://www.library.mmu.ac.uk/bbconnect/ismodel.pdf

Actions and Strategies. When talking with researchers of any age these are very useful discussion points

■ The aged, possibly venerable, but fundamental model first promoted 30 years ago by Michael Marland, chair of a School's Council working group – the Marland Nine Step Model.

Which one do you prefer?

Which one would be most useful to your youngest students?

Which one might be suitable for your older students?

My own favourite start point is still the Marland sequence – it is adaptable and it asks questions of the learner at each stage in the process. We don't have to have nine steps for every enquiry of course – three or four might be enough.[36] We all know that information seeking isn't always sequential. We sometimes revisit different stages depending on challenges and circumstances. But giving secondary school students a linear sequence sets them on their way and gives them confidence, especially when they first start working in this way.

It's always good when schools design and promote their own sequence or particularise one of the popular ones.

See the two case studies at the back of this publication.

Both Lynne Varley and Chris Shercliff have produced their own research sequences/models.

See more from Chris Shercliff in Appendix 5 (p84), also available on the SLA website in the Learning and Teaching section (http://www.sla.org.uk/learning-and-teaching.php).

A Helping Hand with Research is another model used by Liz Smith, librarian at Pembroke School and SLA Board member (see Table 1 opposite).

---

[36] See the SLA Guideline *Cultivating Curiosity* pp17–22 for discussion of using a simple research sequence in a primary school library context.

Table 1.

A Helping Hand with Research.

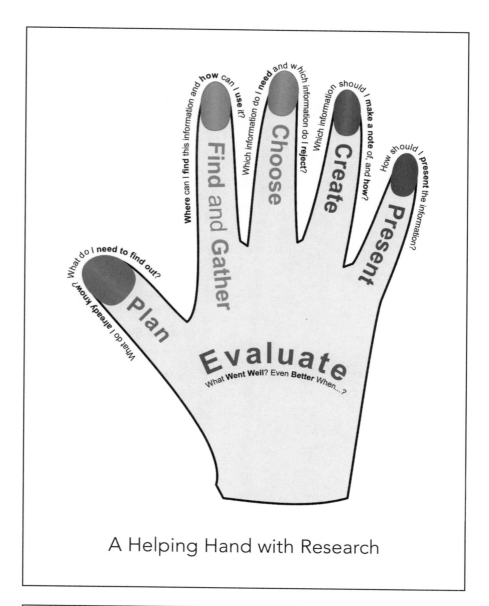

Where can I **find** this information and **how** can I **use** it?

Find and Gather

Which information do I **need** and which information do I **reject**?

Choose

Which information should I **make a note** of, and **how**?

Create

How should I **present** the information?

Present

What do I **need to find out**?

What do I already know?

Plan

Evaluate

What **Went Well**? Even **Better** When...?

A Helping Hand with Research

Based on the John Cabot Academy 'Hand-Up' model.

John Cabot Academy (2004). *Cabot Competency Curriculum: Learning to Learn*. [Online]. [Accessed 13.11.10]. http://www.cabot.ac.uk/index.php/products/ccc/

Smith, Liz (2008). *'Helping Hand' information literacy model*. Pembroke: Pembroke School.

Smith, Sarah. 'INFORM Your Students: Developing an Information Literacy Skills Programme for Year 12 at QEHS'. In: Dubber, Geoff (ed.) (2006). *Sixth Sense: The Sixth Form and the LRC*. Swindon: School Library Association. (pp6–10).

To promote and develop awareness of a steps sequence with learners of any age it is important to:

- talk clearly about the process and encourage the learners to share their ideas and hesitations about information seeking and processing – lesson starters and plenaries are good times for these discussion

- talk about the feelings, the excitement, motivation and stresses of finding out – especially in a school context and the importance of the researcher's information ownership and sense of achievement

- model your own information seeking processes and challenges

- organise the researchers to carry out a simple card sort activity using the step sequence that you wish to promote, or perhaps several of them

- develop a clear sequence for your library and hopefully for the school – perhaps one of the above or one developed for your school with ideas contributed from students and colleagues

- organise the students into groups to produce posters of specific steps in the sequence or to produce a series of footsteps on the floor

- organise them to produce a game for the steps or to use cartoon figures and use a learning journey idea

- publicise the sequence in poster form, as screen savers, on book marks, in student planners, in your library webpages and the school's VLE, in the library, corridors, classrooms, ICT suites and persuade the ICT staff to use the same model.

Now go to the next step – consider how

- any one of these research cycle stages relate to the essential IL target skills that library staff and teachers across the country need to develop

- we might categorise the multitude of sub-skills to make the whole process manageable, indeed intelligible to the learner and deliverable through the curriculum.

See Appendix 1

Look carefully at the table of Research Sequences presented in Appendix 1 (p76). It should give you a clear idea of three well known research cycles/sequences used by effective enquirers, the related target teaching skills and some good examples of the key sub-skills for each one.

Think about the ways in which these skills and concepts relate to the curriculum activities in classrooms across your school.

Chapter Four

Curriculum Capture – the basics

Huge congratulations to all the students on their achievements today and on the hard work of their teachers and parents in achieving what we have done today.

—DfE Nick Gibb, podcast Aug 2010

...It is also important to thank teachers in schools and colleges across the country for their dedication and hard work in preparing their pupils for these very challenging exams.

—DfE Nick Gibb, 'A' Level podcast August 2011

Notice no mention on either occasion of the hard work contributed by library and support staff – they seem invisible to the school's success!

The extent of library staff engagement in information literacy development activities within the school is potentially significant as an indicator of proactive support for students as learners.[37]

Where are you now? Jot down some answers to these two questions...

- *What is your LRC contributing to the general academic success of younger students in school?*

- *What are you contributing to the exam grades awarded to your older students?*

What evidence can you produce to support your thinking?

Information literacy without a curriculum context for the students is of very limited value. The key success criteria is for students to develop and practise the skills across their range of subject areas to promote personal independence, self-confidence, increased motivation and to create a bank of positive experiences with library and internet use and project working. This will take them into further study for education, work and of course leisure too and should also result in increased exam success.

---

[37] CILIP. *School Libraries in the UK: a worthwhile past, a difficult present – and a transformed future.* 2010 p11,
http://www.cilip.org.uk/get-involved/special-interest-groups/school/Documents/full-school-libraries-report.pdf

So how do you start with the curriculum?

If you work in a Local Authority School in England then start here, if you work in an independent school or an Academy that doesn't deliver the National Curriculum to Key Stage 3 students then start at Chapter 5.

If you work in another of the four home countries or elsewhere then clearly you need to access your prescribed curriculum documents.

Do your own investigation/project to find out about your school's curriculum.

Start initially by investigating the curriculum of the younger students: the 11–14 age range.

Start first with English and ICT – these two will be simply overflowing with information literacy concepts, language and potential for the library involvement. See the appropriate website to start your investigation.

- England: http://curriculum.qcda.gov.uk/

If you're using England's curriculum, check out the Key Processes sections first, especially Reading for Meaning (English) and Finding Information, Communicating Information and Evaluating (ICT).

- Wales: http://wales.gov.uk/topics/educationandskills/ schoolshome/curriculuminwales/arevisedcurriculumforwales/ nationalcurriculum/?lang=en
- Scotland: http://www.ltscotland.org.uk/Images/ all_experiences_outcomes_tcm4-539562.pdf
- Northern Ireland: http://www.nicurriculum.org.uk/key_stage_3/

Download target information, highlight key areas of information literacy and retain for reference. This will give you confidence as well as credibility when talking to colleagues in those subject areas and justify your interest in their activities.

Look at this example: read these extracts from the English programme of study for Key Stage 3 and identify the information literacy elements.

2.2 Reading

Reading for meaning

Pupils should be able to:

a extract and interpret information, events, main points and ideas from texts
b infer and deduce meanings, recognising the writers' intentions
c understand how meaning is constructed within sentences and across texts as a whole
d select and compare information from different texts
e assess the usefulness of texts, sift the relevant from the irrelevant and distinguish between fact and opinion
f recognise and discuss different interpretations of texts, justifying their own views on what they read and see, and supporting them with evidence
g understand how audiences and readers choose and respond to texts
h understand how the nature and purpose of texts influences the selection of content and its meanings
i understand how meaning is created through the combination of words, images and sounds in multimodal texts.

Source: http://www.education.gov.uk/schools/teachingandlearning/
curriculum/secondary/b00199101/english/ks3/programme/processes
and
http://media.education.gov.uk/assets/files/pdf/e/english%
202007%20programme%20of%20study%20for%20key%20stage%203.pdf

Now do the same for ICT and then go through the Key Processes all the other subjects. It's also important that you keep up to date with curriculum changes so browse relevant websites on a regular basis.

This will demonstrate the information literacy and library potential for curriculum involvement and give you a clear reason to participate in curriculum planning and general discussion. You have a professional obligation to provide resources for every aspect of your school's curriculum, if anyone asks the reason for your interest!

Now go one step further

If you work with England's National Curriculum at Key Stage 3 take a good look at, download and highlight useful sections of:

- the Framework for Secondary English: overview and learning objectives
  http://www.teachfind.com/national-strategies/framework-secondary-english-strand-overview-and-learning-objectives

- the Framework for Secondary ICT: overview and learning
  http://www.teachfind.com/national-strategies/framework-secondary-ict-strand-overview-and-learning-objectives.

If you work in one of England's Local Authority schools have a go at the following activity using the grid in Table 2 opposite.

Try to identify:

- the secondary school year in which these skill should be taught

- the subject (either English or ICT) for each of these statements from the two frameworks.

The answers are presented in Appendix 2 of this Guideline (p78).

You will immediately be able to identify important information literacy elements and quickly realise that this list contains key parts of a whole school IL programme as well as the progression to make it meaningful.

You can go further and look at the overview and objectives for the other foundation subjects of Maths and Science. To obtain objectives and progression in the subjects beyond English, ICT, Maths and Science is more difficult as the information isn't laid out in the same way – you will need to look at the Level Descriptors for the relevant age groups i.e. Levels 4 to 6.

Note

To avoid a considerable amount of work, do look at the **Information Literacy Checklist** available on the Learning and Teaching section of the SLA website at http://www.sla.org.uk/learning-and-teaching.

You will find that work has been done for you. Information Literacy elements across all subjects have been identified and tabulated in a progressive sequence over the five years of secondary education Y7 – Y11.

able 2.

S Activity: Demonstrating
e Importance of ILS within
e KS3 learning objectives
r English and ICT.

eating an ILS progressive
hool programme.

ENGLISH

Strand 5: Reading for meaning:understanding and responding to print, electronic and multi-modal texts

  5.1 Developing and adapting active reading skills and strategies.

ICT

Strand 1: Finding Information

  1.1 Using data and information sources

National Curriculum learning objective	Year	Subject
Make relevant notes when gathering ideas from texts		
Select information for a task from a range of sources and be aware of the relative strengths and weaknesses of these sources		
Make relevant notes when researching different sources, comparing and contrasting information		
Use a range of reading strategies to retrieve relevant information and main points from a text distinguishing between fact and opinion where appropriate		
Justify the use of particular information sources to support an investigation or presentation and devise and apply criteria to evaluate how well various information types support a task		
Recognise how the content and style of information can influence the message it gives and that data can be distorted or misused		
Acknowledge all sources, recognising copyright and other constraints		
Select from a range of strategies the most appropriate ways to locate, retrieve and compare information and ideas from a variety of texts		
Make relevant notes in a range of formats and approaches when researching a variety of sources		
Collect data systematically from sources for an identified purpose		

If you work in a Local Authority school in England then you will also need to link this to a currently important aspect of curriculum work – the Framework for Personal, Learning and Thinking Skills (P.L.T.S.).[38]

This framework consists of six groups of skills

- independent enquirers
- creative thinkers
- reflective learners
- team workers
- self-managers
- effective participators

Have a good look at them – all are important and provide further clear reasons for cooperation with subject departments.

Whichever routes you have taken so far, at this stage in the information literacy thinking process lots of people are very enthusiastic and decide that an audit of skills across the school would be a good idea. Be careful! I think it better to carry out some curriculum mapping rather than audit work.

Beware audits

Hazards

The following extract is taken from an email I wrote to a colleague in 2010 – an opinion I've held for many years:

> I have seen many (IL skills audits) over the years and usually I have never found them very useful and often they are confusing to the user (perhaps it's just me)! They seem to be take a good deal of time and the end classroom practice (which is their purpose after all!) never seems to be much better.
>
> Let me explain some of the hazards as I see them.
>
> 1) How do you list/structure and define/interpret the skills for a start? This tends to cause confusion before people even start with the mapping process. It is easy to become lost in words and produce lists and charts that people don't understand or don't feel inclined to complete for you. What do you mean by "notetaking?" or "planning" or "brain storming" or "Internet searching with keywords" or even "skim and scan".
>
> 2) When you've produced and circulated a list, the odds are that most people will fill most of them in from their individual subject perspective, rather than from a library or information handling one. This means that answers vary between subjects and you may not gather evidence that is meaningful and therefore helpful.

---

[38] http://www.all-nsc.org.uk/files/PLTS.pdf

3). *Once you have evaluated the results and spotted the gaps in your audit map how do you proceed? Assume there are some gaps in the note taking section or with the understanding of Dewey – do you suggest/tell a dept. to take responsibility for this skill? Do you alert the whole school to the skill, providing a range of suggested strategies for teaching it which colleagues can use as they think fit? Do you as librarian teach these skills during so called "library lessons" without a curriculum context?* [39]

Audits often tend to want to find holes/gaps in what is being taught and people then tend to become defensive. They grumble about other people's responsibilities or about time pressure or suggest they are doing it all already! (and on their terms they may be – who can argue?).

To change practice and make progress you need to use other strategies. To develop whole school thinking school librarians need to have:

- Time
- Motivation
- Positive feedback and reassurance
- The option to use a variety of strategies to suit particular needs
- The flexibility to use a certain amount of trial and error
- The confidence to use regular evaluation and reflection.

The secret is to sell IL as making learning more effective and motivating – not as something extra and threatening.

---

[39] part extract of 2010 email sent to a colleague, based on similar over the last decade

Chapter Five

Curriculum Capture – school topics

If you work in an independent school or perhaps in an Academy, or if you work outside England then this might be your start point as your school might not follow England's National Curriculum.

A word of advice – as a general rule avoid asking busy Heads of Faculty/ Departments for their schemes of work. Usually response levels are low and information if you receive it may confuse rather than clarify and even if you obtain enough information you still need to organise it in some way.

An effective way to visualise and organise the curriculum is to build your own series of curriculum maps. I have introduced this mapping to many librarians over the last two decades – it is an excellent way to gain a useful overview.

You may find most of the relevant information on your school's virtual learning platform or intranet, but I still advise you to talk to subject departments about the detail.

Data gathering activity

1. Use a large piece of flipchart paper or sugar paper (you will ultimately need six of them – assuming six half-terms in any academic school year). This data gathering can of course be done by digital means, but many people find the process of actual and practical collection interesting and more memorable. You are initially going to gather information on the 11–14 (Key Stage 3) curriculum, if you feel ambitious then gather information for the upper school too, but you will have the complication of exam syllabuses to consider.

2. Divide your first sheet into sections as follows:

Autumn Term 1	Year 7	Year 8	Year 9
English			
Maths			
History			
Geography			
Science			
etc.			

3. Now complete as much of the table as you can by talking to teachers, students, observation etc. – it may be useful to use post-it notes or similar in the first instance. You will inevitably have some gaps – no matter at this stage.

4. I suggest that you use two different colours to compile your various curriculum maps – one colour to indicate library (and library resource use) for a topic, e.g. you know that the geographers always do a piece of investigative/project work on rivers in Year 8 and use library resources. Another colour to indicate that library (and library resource) use is very unlikely, e.g. the Maths Dept is doing a topic on quadratic equations.

5. Once you know with some certainty the topics being taught to different year groups across the school by the various departments, so skills for each year (see the list in the Learning and Teaching section of the SLA website: http://www.sla.org.uk/learning-and-teaching.php) can be targeted through appropriate topics – you and teacher working in partnership.

How successful has this activity been?

Jot down some notes for the next occasion.

This will have given you a general overview of the 11–14 curriculum, enough to do some resource planning and preparation and to start considering IL in a wider context. You have:

- the skills to be taught to each year as outlined in the National Curriculum and
- the important school topics for each part of each year.

You now need ways to link them together and offer your services to teaching colleagues.

Now you have a general overview of the Lower School work, what next – where do you want to start making an impact?
Year 7 as the new intake year?
or
Years 10 and 11 – perhaps more needs to be achieved at GCSE level
or
Years 12 and 13: the Sixth Form? The transfer to 16–19 exam work is one of the biggest academic jumps that students make, taking on new subjects, working much more privately and independently and using a range of texts far above those used lower down the school.

Working with the new Year 7 students

In order to do this you will need to do the following:

- Learn something about the Year 6 curriculum across your range of partner primary schools

- Learn something about the library and information literacy experience of children from those schools

- Develop an effective initial library induction package for those new intake students. This could perhaps be started in the last few weeks of their primary schooling and completed at the start of the new academic years, aiding a successful transition.

It's important to realise that the induction package isn't an introduction to information literacy but merely allows the children to become familiar with their new library. This means that they should find it easier to use their new library productively and confidently which in turn should provide a good foundation for IL teaching and learning. To obtain some ideas for successful library induction for Y7s, and indeed other years and adults as well, see the relevant SLA Guideline.[40]

Working with the 14–16 students – the exam classes

Here again a library/IL induction package may well be helpful for students starting out on these life changing exams.

You will need to obtain a working knowledge of the key GCSE and exam syllabuses by locating information on relevant exam board websites, talking to your school's exams officer and to teaching colleagues to discover options, controlled assessment details and requirements for individual courses. The reading lists provided by exam boards may also be helpful to you.

Again drawing up or extending your lower school curriculum maps of this information may well prove very useful as you consider IL strategies and the resources that you can offer.

14–16

Ways to support IL across the 14–16 age range include:

Y10

- By induction at the beginning of Y10 that focuses on the new opportunities that the LRC can offer to support exam controlled assessment

- By being 'in the know' about the timing and details of major pieces of work and having resources ready to support it. By helping the student

---

[40] SLA Guideline *Crossing the Divide* by Geoff Dubber (2009).

to make links to the information world beyond school – local library, business, industry

- By having in stock examples/ models – perhaps as photocopies, of good coursework

- By having lots of local data, information, maps etc. on easy access

- By accessing some E-learning ILS materials

- By reinforcing your earlier messages about copyright issues, plagiarism, referencing skills, note making

- By producing some hard copy or digital guidance on key issues such as time management, essay writing, referencing and citation, on-line resources.

See the excellent booklet *Independent Learning Guides* (SLA Voices) produced by Dominique Collins, librarian at Hurstpierpoint College on the SLA website at http://www.sla.org.uk/sla-voices.

Y11

- By keeping in stock a range of subject based revision guides – to borrow or as reference material and having a collection of past papers

- By linking up with work being done by the school's Careers Education/Connexions – information for Further/Higher Education etc.

- By liaising with the local library service about forthcoming assessment pieces

- By teacher partnership study support clinics and LRC based revision sessions and providing lists of useful weblinks

- And again by providing some e-learning ILS materials for those who want to use it

- Giving reminders of dates and details for controlled assessment etc. on your plasma screen, VLE etc.

16–19 Working with the 16–19 students

As with the 14–16 age range, a library/IL induction package might be useful and if you want to become familiar with the curriculum you will need to draw up or extend your existing lower school series of curriculum maps, again recording details of various exam boards used, exams sat, options taken, quantities of course work produced and the related administration. At that point you can again offer your services and IL expertise to these students.

At what ever level you are working, your credibility as a librarian and an IL expert will be very much enhanced if you can talk curriculum with your students. Without that knowledge they will take much less interest in

your work and your impact on their study habits and IL development will be much the poorer.

As Anne Robinson at The Dixie Grammar School stated so clearly on her blog in April 2009, many students:

- Do not understand how to appraise resources
- Have not gone beyond Google in search engines
- Have never used a subscription database
- Have never used journals
- Have never read around their subject
- Are shaky when it comes to writing essays
- Have issues with plagiarism
- Have issues around understanding what a library is – a shared public space
- They also have issues around security – belongings, passwords, library cards etc.

There is much IL work to do with many of these students if they are to achieve their best.

Ways that you might support IL across the 16–19 age range include:

- By producing an effective induction package in cooperation with Sixth Form tutors that looks at the variety of resources, exam requirements and effective study habits that students will need in order to be successful
- By producing some hard copy or digital guidance on key issues such as time management, essay writing, referencing and citation, on-line resources. See the excellent booklet *Independent Learning Guides* (SLA Voices) produced by Dominique Collins, librarian at Hurstpierpoint College on the SLA website at http://www.sla.org.uk/sla-voices
- By teaching them to use the various varied services offered by Google – Google Scholar, Google search help
- By demonstrating the use of other search engines, Intute (closed July 2011 so not updated) etc.
- By pointing the students to a whole range of excellent e-learning IL websites in the UK and wider

- Organising visits to university and HE libraries and other information locations – archives, museums, major reference libraries etc.

- Giving one to one guidance on a range of study habits and revision techniques

- By holding past papers – yes digital copies are available, but having them to hand makes a world of difference and shows that you've looked at them too

- Posting dates and details of course work on your plasma screen website, bulletin boards.

Note any ideas for working with the 14–16 or 16+ age ranges that you can usefully follow up.

Chapter Six

Working with Teaching and Learning Support Colleagues

I wonder if anyone can help me. I'm having a hard job convincing some of my English staff that research should not mean Googling and copy and pasting from Wikipedia.[41]

I actually ran (my IL ideas) past the Head of ICT at school... but have now been waiting 16 months for the Leadership Team to give me the opportunity to tell the rest of the staff about it. It makes me mad. They keep harping on about the importance of Literacy but can't find me 15 minutes. Grrrrr! Anyway, enough of my ranting![42]

It has been demonstrated that when librarians and teachers work together, students achieve higher levels of literacy, reading, learning, problem solving and information and communications technology skills.[43]

We all know that school library staff are betwixt and between – not officially seen as teachers, although the professional qualifications of many are equal to those of many teachers. You are concerned with the curriculum on a daily, often hourly basis, yet your expertise and vision isn't wholly recognised. Often working as a one person band, and not usually more than a team of two, you frequently find yourself outside the curriculum decision-making forum and sometimes even managed by a support team manager rather than a curriculum director.

To add to the challenge you often attempt to work with colleagues who don't understand your expertise and whose working environs, the classroom, is often difficult for you to access and if and when they do visit your library with classes or small groups they need the space rather than school library expertise – you may feel unable to offer intervention strategies or effective help.

Remember the quote from Henry Ford:

If you always do what you've always done, you'll always get what you always got!

---

[41] plea on a school library listserv in 2010.
[42] email from a colleague, November 2009.
[43] IFLA/UNESCO School Library manifesto
http://archive.ifla.org/VII/s11/pubs/manifest.htm Acessed 18 Oct. 2011.

For further information, see *Awareness and Promotion of Information Literacy* (2011) by Pat Cowley, a publication from the SLA in the Voices series – http://www.sla.org.uk/sla-voices.php

Do remember the importance of IL 'embeddedness' at all levels. Discrete IL lessons, run by library staff, however well meaning, really aren't very effective.

> *IL training should be embedded within the subject curriculum to maximize relevance, timeliness and student motivation. Stand-alone sessions are less effective: it can be difficult for a learner to transfer a skill practised in a generic environment into a subject specific context.*[44]

Or

> *IL needs to be embedded into the academic curriculum as far as possible; it also needs to be ongoing throughout a student's academic career and adapted according to the specific requirements of the discipline.*[45]

Working with teaching colleagues

Some useful strategies.

Once you have learned something of their curriculum responsibilities and content:

■ Meet with them on a regular basis to know their curriculum thinking and needs. You may need to close the library while you do this – perhaps one break time a week.

> *I used to open the LRC before and after school and at lunchtimes, but break was my time to informally network. It was invaluable both professionally and personally. Just getting out there and being 'seen' and having a chance to socialise too, otherwise it's very isolating.*[46]

■ Talk curriculum, skills and library with them on a regular basis so they appreciate your knowledge, interests and expertise. They expect you to know about children's literature and books, but talk IL as well.

■ Of course you'll invite them to use the library resources, perhaps borrow loan boxes from your own stock or/and from your local Schools Library Service. Try to get into the classroom when those resources are being used – you will learn a great deal about the topic being taught, classroom management techniques and policies and the suitability of the actual texts being used.

---

[44] Cardiff University, Handbook for Information Literacy teaching July 2009, p3.
[45] Secker and Coonan, 2011. *A New Curriculum for Information Literacy*. Executive Summary, p6. Arcadia Project.
[46] Comment from Claire Larson 28/10/2011

- Produce a leaflet offering your library services to them – if they use the library this is what you can offer (and what you expect too). A leaflet can develop clear expectations on both sides and reduce misunderstandings.

- Try to make sure that every teacher who uses the library completes a booking form for you (hopefully and necessarily 24 hours before). You need this in order to prepare resources for the visit, organise seating, warn other users, discover the learning objectives for the session and negotiate your participation in it. You need a sample of these forms for your self-evaluation evidence too.[47]

- If on the other hand the teacher is only using the space then this information needs to be recorded too as the school may need more classroom space and this action is putting unwelcome pressure on library space.

- Make sure that small group and personal study use for the 11–16 age range is directed. This can be achieved by requiring that all researches from the lower school (unless booked with an organised class group) come with a completed research slip. Those that don't are asked to return to the classroom.

A research slip records the following details:

✔ Name of student, class and teacher

✔ Date and time

✔ Question(s) to be researched (you can't research a topic it may take a life time!)

✔ Suggested resources

✔ Action to be taken on discovery of relevant information

✔ Teacher's signature

It will also contain the library's logo as it is was originally issued from the library to the teaching departments and will remind everyone of the library's role.

It is the main communication between you, the teacher and the student. Sometimes students are unclear as to the purpose of their visit. It clearly shows the reason why the student is visiting the library rather than remaining in the classroom.

---

[47] See SLA Guideline *Quality and Impact: Evaluating the Performance of your School Library* (2011).

You will need a sample of these slips, along with copies of research work and IL work to show your own and the library's 'added value' to a selection of student work. It helps to demonstrate your contribution to learning.

Of course it is important to be flexible and welcome laissez-faire use too. The library should always be seen as relaxed and welcoming. It is also important that users see it as a serious contributor to teaching and learning and not simply a bolt hole from lessons! This same principle also applies to Sixth Form Private Study use.

Which of those on the list do you use already?

Make a note of others that might work for you.

Working with support staff colleagues

Support staff work in a wide variety of ways in all schools, but many use the library for small group mentoring/nurturing work or assisting students with research type activities. It's important that they appreciate your expertise and potential to help them and their students and that they feel part of the library ethos.

Some useful strategies include:

- Provide library induction for all new support staff, whether or not they will use the library as part of their responsibilities
- Encourage them to share agreed library practices and policies
- Make sure they feel welcome to borrow books and the wider range of resources that you offer
- Make sure that their use with small groups is recorded in the same way as teachers with classes. All use should be visible to show the amount of work that you do and the continual pressure on the LRC and its resources.

Working with student teachers

Many schools welcome ITT or PGCE students. Enthusiastic and committed, these future teachers are often a prime captive audience for some hard sell about library use and IL teaching and learning ideas. As part of your induction package for these transitory groups talk about IL, share your policy ideas and get them involved. Their experiences of their own school libraries will still be fresh, their opinions of working in an HE setting even more current but their IL expertise may need some finesse.

Working with students as they research

If possible get involved at the planning stage of curriculum activities. If you know some of the curriculum objectives, provide obvious enthusiasm and expertise and ideas and can offer an exciting range of resources your teaching and support staff colleagues will see you as a superstar! You'll make their life easier and using the library and its resources will become an intrinsic part of their planning process. This takes time to achieve, but IL skills can then be built into the early stage of curriculum planning and you are more likely to become a key partner in the teaching and learning process.

Initially though a good deal of your work with research tasks is likely to be hasty and reactive. Students arrive at the library, probably at short notice, and require instant attention and immediately accessible information!

They may be uncertain about the information needs or time schedule demands of the task or the research steps that they need to take to be successful.

Research tasks tend to miss the target if:

- The task is too closed
  - e.g. *What is the distance between the earth and the sun?*

- The task is too complex and lacks a clear a pathway
  - e.g. *Homework tonight is find out all you can about Icelandic volcanoes.*

- Time allocation is unreasonable or too vague
  - e.g. *I want you to do a project in the next five homeworks.*

- Resource guidance is poor
  - e.g. *Go to the library and find out about Winston Churchill as Britain's wartime prime minister.*

Consider these tasks set to Y7 students and faced by school library staff a few months ago:

1. Find information about how we have evolved from apes. Describe part of the evolution process with the information that you find.

2. Find out about William Shakespeare and his life. Who was he? What did he do? When did he live? What was life like when he was alive?

3. The homework I have set for this week is to 'Research Phobias'. Obviously, this is quite open-ended and should provoke some interesting responses...

Which one might be the most difficult?

Which IL skills will the students by most likely to learn from these activities?

How successful are the students likely to be?

How would you help a group who came to you with any of these tasks?

What advice would you offer to a teaching colleagues who offered any of these tasks?

Successful IL research activities/project type work start with:

- Effective task setting
- Sharing clear teaching/learning objectives
- Activating prior knowledge
- Time management discussion
- Sharing of assessment criteria
- Discussion of search terms/keywords
- Possibly modelling to demonstrate completed work or skills to be used
- Sharing/reinforcing/developing the research cycle/sequence.

We need to be able to prompt teaching and support staff colleagues to consider these basic points, and either make the research very clear or deliberately leave details to the learner.

We need our learners to be sure of these points before starting out on their research journey. With this information they will be all the more likely to finish successfully and confidently.

Table 3 overleaf presents a prompt list that could be used by whoever is planning the student project/research activity.

Table 3.

Decisions to be made at the planning stage	Teacher decides	Pupil/Group decides
Overall learning objectives linked to school's curriculum		
Subject area of research		
Title/question to research		
Amount of time needed for each stage of the work		
Handing in date/time		
Balance of time between 'finding out' and presenting		
Deciding on a learning path		
Possible Information locations and access		
Type/number of resources to use		
Organising and recording information methods to be used		
Ways to process the information/answer the question		
Presentation style and format for the intended audience		
Evaluation/assessment method/criteria to be used		

As students become more effective researchers, so more decisions can be left to their discretion. You can make a progression of guidance here – clearly your A2 students doing examination Extended Project type work should be better able to make decisions than your Y9s who, in turn should need less teacher direction that the new intake Y7s.

To go one step further than a research cycle for an extended piece of research work, then provide a project planner for your students – perhaps linked to a specific piece of work in a friendly department in the first instance, but later consider a more generic project planner that all departments can use/adapt as required and can link to library practices.

A project planner clearly needs to fit the abilities and attitudes of the students and the complexity of the research task, but consider using some of the following sections which can reflect a research cycle/sequence in format.

The student completes each stage in a space provided as part of the learning journey and the planner is graded/marked along with subject content:

- Details of student/group – name(s), class, teacher
- Library logo
- Diary of progress made in the work
- Completion date
- Time management details
- Title of question/investigation
- Marking criteria for the content and the project planner
- Presentation method
- Prior knowledge
- Suitable key words and Dewey numbers
- Key resources/websites to consult and perhaps the ones to use first
- Advice offered by library staff
- Ways to assess the validity of the information
- Ways to collect information
- Reminder to use simple non-fiction writing tools – contents page, chapters, subheadings, citations, footnotes, glossary, reading list etc.
- Ways to process the information
- Evaluation thoughts.

Nicola Mason, librarian at Wilmslow High in Cheshire devised one for her school to link closely with the Personal Learning and Thinking Skills framework outlined by the DfE[48] and promoted in her school, as she put in her email:

> At the moment it is only used with groups that are brought into the LRC, but I am liaising with the deputy head to get a version in our student planners next academic year.

Her sample project planner is shown on pp46–47.

Nicola also used a very useful *Where Do I Start?* sheet (see Appendix 6, p85) that asks students to activate their prior knowledge on their research topic and then turn key words into essentials questions – the basis of all good research.

---

[48] this information is no longer obvious on the DfE website but a good explanation can be found at http://www.all-nsc.org.uk/files/PLTS.pdf (Accessed 5 Mar. 2012)

Project Planner

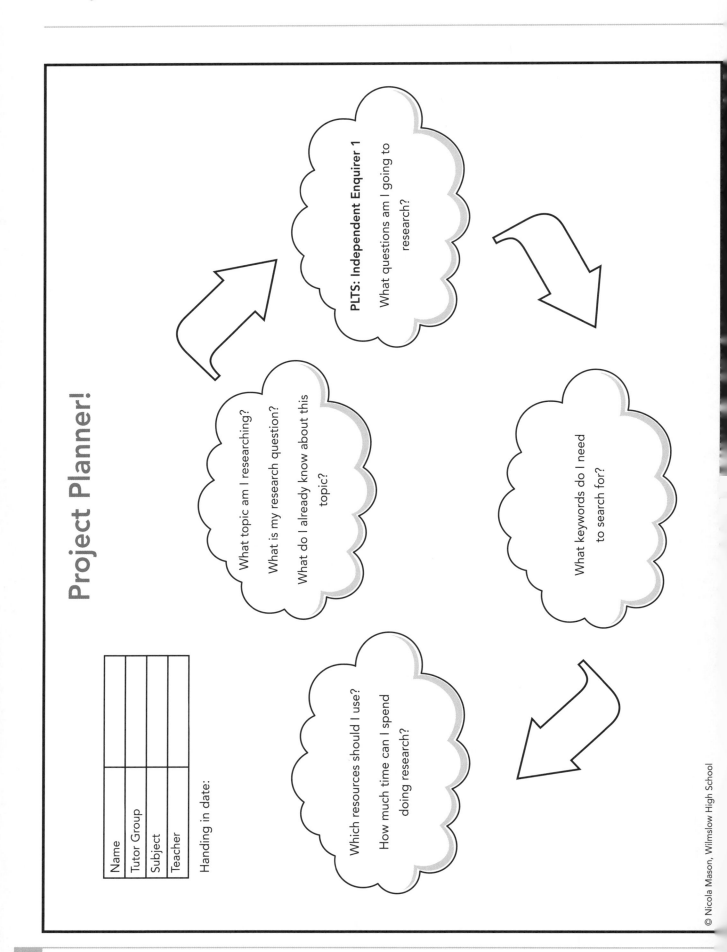

Start Your Research!

List the resources you use
(give the names and authors
of books and websites)

PLTS: Independent Enquirer 4

Which resource was the easiest to use?

Which resource had the most information?

Which resource was the most useful?

PLTS: Reflective Learner

Now you need to think about:

- Have I collected enough information?

- How am I going to present my work?

- How can I make sure this is my best work?

Make sure you check your work!

Write down two new things you have learnt:

Write down two skills you have used:

Chapter Seven

Assessment issues

Information literate pupils:
Know which questions are useful to ask
Are independent readers, skimming and scanning to find what they need
Know what is relevant, can select and reject information
Read texts in different ways for different purposes
Know when they have found enough information
Make relevant notes and use them to support classwork and homework
Synthesise and combine information from a variety of sources
Cross-refer and compare information from a variety of sources
Re-present information coherently, demonstrating understanding and learning
Evaluate their sources
Evaluate their work and reflect on their learning.

—DfES, 2004

Assessment of IL is as important as its planning, partnership working with teaching colleagues and its delivery. It is a key part of the teaching and learning cycle.

Key questions to ask yourself:

- How well are my students doing?
- How much progress have they made because of the work I am doing?
- What do they feel about their progress?
- What aspects of the research process and information processing do they find most difficult?
- How does that information affect what I do?
- How do my colleagues in school learn about my input and the progress the students are making with IL generally and with library use

Understanding the progress being made by your students as you work with them in both formal (class learning) and informal (free time and homework club) settings will help your own self-evaluation thoughts and inform your promotion and development planning activities too.

How well teachers assess their pupils' progress and then use the information they gather to improve their learning are critical in the overall quality of teaching.[49]

---

[49] Extract from Christine Gilbert's *HMCI Annual Report Education, Children and Skills 2009/10* http://www.ofsted.gov.uk/about-us/annual-report

Clearly the same could be said of library staff involved in IL delivery. Assessment goes hand in hand with progression.

Assess the benefits of your library induction package

Most library staff deliver an induction package[50] to the new intake year, the 14+ and 16+ students and new colleagues in school that has some element of IL in it.

- What did the students learn from it?
- How do you know?
- How did you reward them?
- How will your findings affect the next induction package and your follow up ILS work?

This can be discovered by providing quiz sheets, structured activities, observation and evaluation sheets.

Remember to provide positive feedback for any assessment that you do to boost student confidence and understanding and also to inform your line manager.

Table 4.

The assessment cycle

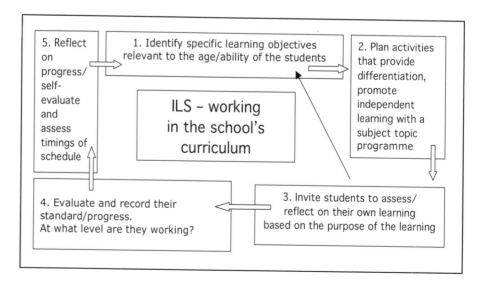

---

[50] To gain ideas for library induction see SLA Guideline *Crossing the Divide: LRC Induction and Transition Strategies* http://www.sla.org.uk/guidelines

It is useful to remember that the best assessment is achieved when the learner evaluates his/her own success and can see progression in their own personal learning.

Assessment can be carried out in two ways:

1. Formative Assessment (ongoing) – self help type reflection that helps the student to check their understanding and judge their skills level

2. Summative assessment – used by the teacher/library staff to judge a student at the end of a unit before passing on to a new module (eg a formal test).

Three possibilities for formative assessment are:

1. Self-assessment

This can be done by providing a simple checklist of skills and asking the students to score themselves against set criteria. Do this in a relaxed and fairly informal way so that you receive reasonably honest answers. See also the ideas suggested by Anne-Marie Tarter and Anne Robinson.[51]

2. Peer assessment

When students give positive guidance and grades to their own work and those of their classmates.

> It is much more than children marking their own or each other's work... it must be an activity that engages children with the quality of their work helps them reflect on how to improve it. Peer assessment enables children to give each other valuable feedback so they learn from and support each other. It adds a valuable dimension to learning: the opportunity to talk, discuss, explain and challenge each other enables children to achieve beyond what they can learn unaided. Peer assessment helps develop self-assessment, which promotes independent learning, helping children to take increasing responsibility for their own progress.[52]

Visualisers can be very helpful here too – to display a piece of work for the entire group to see, enabling the class to discuss its merits and possible areas for improvement.[53]

In order to give reasoned opinions and helpful comments about the quality of their work and that of others, all the students will need to have a shared understanding of the teaching/learning objectives and so they will need a mark or grade guide.

---

[51] http://www.ebase.bcu.ac.uk/projects/schoollibraries.htm (accessed 7/9/2011)

[52] quoted from the DfE's *Assessment for Learning* materials, now archived in June 2011. http://nationalstrategies.standards.dcsf.gov.uk/node/18700?uc = force_uj

[53] http://www.guardian.co.uk/education/2008/jan/08/link.link16

Try this simple class/group activity:

- One pair/group shows another how to do something – locate a resource, locate some information, use a search engine effectively, make some notes, cite a source etc.

- The other group comments on/grades the performance. Then they reverse roles

- Whole class discussion to draw out successes and challenges.

There are several peer and self-assessment templates available on the internet, see in particular the useful work of Fiona Hogg.[54]

3. **Librarian assessment**

This can be achieved in many ways during and at the end of a lesson. The most popular are using question and answer techniques, by effective use of the plenary at the end of a session, by constant observation and by one to one discussions and mentoring. A fund of other ideas to help you can be found at:

http://office.microsoft.com/enus/templates/ CT010281918.aspx?tl=2#pg:7lai:TC001212023l

http://daretodifferentiate.wikispaces.com/file/view/03+- +Formative+Assessment+Strategies.pdf

http://www.taosschools.org/ths/School%20Improvement/CIEDipTTModule7Ty pesofFormativeAssessment.pdf

If you're looking at your students' use of the research cycle/sequence then you might like to measure each student in one of three categories:

- Emergent/Beginner

- Established/Proficient

- Advanced/Confident.

See Lewis M. and Wray D. (eds). *Literacy in the Secondary School* (2000) Chap 4. David Fulton for an excellent chart.

Also take a look at the Prince Edward Island website – *Building Information Literacy: Strategies for Developing Informed Decision-Makers and Independent Lifelong Learners* – Student Learning Outcomes section.[55]

---

[54] http://www.fionahogg.com/Unit%2012a%20Self%20and%20peer%20assess.pdf Accessed 7 Sep. 2011.
[55] http://www.edu.pe.ca/bil/ Accessed 19 Mar. 2012.

Certainly if you work in a Local Authority school in England it is very useful to be able to ascertain the National Curriculum level at which the student is working.

See Appendix 3

The table in Appendix 3 (p79) is taken from National Curriculum level statements shows progression in Reading Skills from Y3 to Y8. Compare your students' work to the progressive statements.

It is also useful to chart progress against levels in ICT as much of that too is basic IL. Knowing the level at which your students are performing for specific IL tasks is a real asset when talking general and individual student progress with the students themselves, colleagues and parents. It is also useful to know the level of ICT skills that you can expect students to apply to tasks that you set them. Taking this further into 14+ and 16+ controlled assessment and coursework is also helpful. Check out the marking criteria on the relevant exam board website for further ideas.[57]

---

[57] For example see marking Criteria (essentially IL work) for the AQA Extended Project Qualification Level 3 at http://www.diplomainfo.org.uk/documents/AQA EPQ-W-SP-07-08.pdf Accessed 7 Sept. 2011

Chapter Eight

'They only use Google and Wikipedia'

In this world of the Internet and other readily accessible digital information, the use of scholarly documents has plummeted and the use of undependable Web resources has soared.[58]

What's your favourite search engine and why?

Which ones do you use on a regular basis?

What's your attitude to Wikipedia

ILS and the Web are clearly inseparable, but teaching our students to employ a range of strategies rather than simply typing a rather general search term/keyword into Google or using Wikipedia and expecting a quick fix answer is important. Like all of us, our students employ strategies to get to the answer in the shortest possible time – that's often how the brain works – task completion is often paramount, if the product rather than the method is seen as the more important.

Working with your teaching and support colleagues, use some of the following strategies to build their search strategies and IL competency:

- Tasks can specify the use of different resources on the basis that the finding out is as equally important as the result. By all means allow students to start with Wikipedia and then demand use of other resources too. Wikipedia often provides an excellent overview of a topic, especially for those with limited prior knowledge. Many people use it for straightforward simple information enquiries, but often effective learning is a good deal more than finding a simple answer.

- Teach students to use Google effectively. Let them try a range of Google activities.[59]

- Take a look at the 2006 Google Game, its update and the commentary created by a school librarian in Pennsylvania to give you more ideas.[60]

---

[58] Quoted in *Cite Them Right*, Richard Pears and Graham Shield, page iii
[59] http://blogoscoped.com/archive/2006-08-13-n15.html Accessed 18 Oct. 2011. http://www.makeuseof.com/tag/7-quick-casual-google-search-games/ Accessed 18 Oct. 2011.
[60] http://www.schoollibraryjournal.com/article/CA6296500.html http://www.schoollibraryjournal.com/article/CA6555545.html?q=return+of+the+google+game Accessed 18 Oct. 2011.

- Take a look at Four Nets for Better Searching[61] – to quote the website *If you make a habit of using the four techniques described below, you'll be a much better searcher than 90% of all web-users.*

  The Four Nets are – start Narrow, find Exact Phrases, Trim back the URL, seek Similar Pages.

- Make sure students cite/reference resources used. Part of the mark scheme for an activity can involve citing creating a list of references or a bibliography – to the school's/the library's preferred method.

  The standard school way to cite sources can become a whole school policy from the new intake year onwards and failure to use it can then result in reduced marks or grades.

- Displays of information can include hard copy and digital copy alongside each other.

- Suggested reading on topic bookmarks produced by library staff to promote locating and gathering skills and resource familiarity. This can include both hard copy and digital references/images.

- Encourage competition between groups to identify information at speed, making sure that the digital/Google group doesn't always win.

- Encourage them to produce Wikipedia type entries on aspects of their work – the peer review, discussion and altering can lead to genuine debate and become an important part of the learning process.

- Encourage the use of online journals, especially with older students. Why not buy into JCS Online Resources or join one of the local consortia, perhaps through your School Library Service, accessing a range of digital reference material? Alternatively work in partnership with your local library where access to many of these resources will be freely available.

- Talk about the size of the Web with students – create some posters, put up some displays about information growth and projections.

- Remind them that according to JISC, *The Web expands at an astonishing rate. Statistics suggest that more than 70 new domains are registered and more than 500,000 documents are added to the web every minute.*[62]

And there are a good deal more to be located and used in the 'hidden web'.[63]

Searching on the Internet today can be compared to dragging a net across the surface of the ocean. There is a wealth of information that is deep, and therefore missed...

[61] http://webquest.sdsu.edu/searching/fournets.htm Accessed 18 Oct. 2011
[62] http://www.jisc.ac.uk/events/2011/10/futureoftheweb.aspx Accessed 29 Sept. 2011
[63] following extracts from *The Deep Web – Surfacing Hidden Value.* Bright Planet Corporation July 2000, last updated Oct 2009. http://www.brightplanet.com/images/uploads/DeepWebWhitePaper_20091015. pdf Accessed 29 Sept. 2011

> ■ ■ *Public information on the deep Web is currently 400 to 550 times larger than the commonly defined World Wide Web*
>
> ■ ■ *The deep Web contains nearly 550 billion individual documents compared to the 1 billion of the surface Web.*

We all know that finding more isn't necessarily finding better but being aware that Google won't necessarily find you the answer you need is important.

Further strategies to consider:

■ Make sure that students practise using a range of search engines and search tools, through clear task instructions. Ask groups to compare search engine results. Become familiar yourself with some of those Keyword, Index, Meta, Visual and Category search engines listed by Phil Bradley,[64] or to go further have a look at the search tools listed on the Infopeople site[65] and of course use the popular Noodletools site of Debbie and Damon Abilock.[66]

■ Encourage your older students to use subject gateways – Pinakes http://www.hw.ac.uk/libwww/irn/pinakes/pinakes.html with its wide range of sites will interest those who want more sophisticated information.

■ Teach web evaluation skills and criteria. This is a vital aspect of the school's librarian's work as an information specialist.

For younger students, use of Kathy Shrock's '5 Ws' is excellent.[67] Ask them to create their own posters and evaluate websites on topics before they start using them. Use spoof websites too of course and encourage students to make up spoof information to fool their peers. Those whose information remains undiscovered the longest are the winners! For older students use the PROMPT checklist available on the Open University Learning Space site.[68]

It is so important that students don't take all information as reliable. Encourage them to look at sites where information is likely to be one-sided - such as badger culling, fox hunting, veal meat production, circus animals, wind farms, transport policy – the H2S High Speed Rail link, totalitarian regimes in the Middle East, or other websites that discuss controversial or sensitive issues.

Also ask your students to investigate the sites of the main UK political parties and of course sites about aliens and UFOs as these always provide a wealth of interesting (and controversial) material.

---

[64] http://www.philb.com/whichengine.htm Accessed 29 Sept. 2011
[65] http://infopeople.org/search/chart Accessed 29 Sept. 2011
[66] http://www.noodletools.com/debbie/literacies/information/5locate/adviceengine.html Accessed 29 Sept. 2011
[67] http://kathyschrock.net/abceval/5ws.htm Accessed 29 Sept 2011
[68] http://openlearn.open.ac.uk/mod/oucontent/view.php?id=397525andsection=1.7.1 Accessed 29 Sept. 2011

Chapter Nine

The next step

We need to be at the forefront of the 2.0 movement in our libraries, championing the content and trialling the tools to exploit their teaching potential.[69]

I think my motto is: libraries aren't going away; old libraries are going away.[70]

We are on the cusp of huge change in school libraries, brought about by the advent of new and exciting technologies. Some commentators suggest that we try to avoid the term Web.2.0 – outdated they suggest – and think instead of the range of possibilities such as:

- social networking
- mobile learning
- smart technologies/devices
- personalised learning
- e-learning
- augmented reality
- multi-media

The term isn't important, the way that school library staff adapt to use these technologies and concepts to support the information seeking and handling activities of their students and staff colleagues certainly will be.

We are still struggling over use of mobile phones in schools. The technology has outrun the administrative systems for safeguarding students and teachers. School library staff understand the importance of mobile technology to the research process yet must operate within rather outdated school policies and practices.

Just interested in your opinions as we have a complete ban on mobile phones... for me this doesn't sound like a great idea.[71]

---

[69] Peter Godwin and Jo Parker (2008) *Information Literacy meets Library 2.0.* p.8 Facet Publishing

[70] http://doug-johnson.squarespace.com/blue-skunk-blog/2010/6/17/close-the-library-guest-post-by-r-cicchetti.html. Accessed 17 Oct. 2011

[71] email on a listserv from a colleague on the SLA Board. Nov. 2010

One very positive response was

> I am a great fan of mobile phones in teaching and learning. I can't believe that anyone would seriously consider banning them in this day and age... An IT manager pointed out that we don't ban pencils and pens just because someone might stab someone else with one! Mobiles are a way of life these days. I get students to record their thoughts on reading paragraphs from books or webpages, older students can take pictures of bibliographic details of sources they have used... (anything) to prevent them getting bored and having their ideas stifled just with the act of writing.[72]

> Give students smartphones to boost education standards, say experts: Academics argue that the handheld devices are vital if British pupils are to compete internationally.[73]

Clearly though school library staff do need to be aware of safeguarding and student conduct issues, and come to terms with the more traditional views of libraries. We need to be prepared to invest time to become familiar and confident with using this wide range of applications and software.

See Appendix 4

Appendix 4 (p80) shows a list of interesting and useful tools to support the specific 'umbrella' IL skills.[74] It is also available in the Learning and Teaching section of the SLA website: http://www.sla.org.uk/learning-and-teaching.php

Appendix 4: A sample of appropriate freeware tools

IL Key Target Skill	Freeware tool example
Planning	**Get organised** Toodledo http://www.toodledo.com Get organized with a to-do list – also available for the iPhone **Generate ideas** WiseMapping http://www.wisemapping.com Generate and organize your ideas in visual formats Mindmeister www.mindmeister.com Edraw Mind Map http://www.edrawsoft.com/freemind.php Free Mind http://freemind.sourceforge.net/wiki/index.php/Main_Page **Revision Planner** BBC Revision Planners http://www.bbc.co.uk/schools/studentlife/ revisionandskills/revisionwisksm_planners.shtml
Locating & Gathering	**Bookmark web sites** Delicious http://delicious.com Store, organize and share all your bookmarks. **Organize your stuff online** Netvibes http://www.netvibes.com Create a personalized homepage and add widgets to organize your stuff online **Collaborate with others** Voicethread http://voicethread.com "Group conversations around images, documents and videos" **Carry out a survey** SurveyMonkey http://www.surveymonkey.com Design a survey, collect responses and analyse your results.

[72] thoughts from Sarah Pavey, Librarian at Box Hill School. Nov 2010

[73] Headlines from an article in MSP News 30 Oct. 2011
http://www.mspnews.com/news/2011/10/30/5893381.htm Accessed 2 Nov. 2011

[74] Thanks to Caroline Roche and Lesley Watts for sharing some of the sites with colleagues on the School Librarian Listserv.

> **With which of these tools are you familiar?**
>
> **Which is your favourite?**
>
> **Which one might you investigate next?**

To go further with some of these tools have a look at two excellent resources:

- *The Amazing Web 2.0 Projects Book* ed. by Terry Freedman – 120+ pages of interesting material and a fund of good ideas[75]

- The SLA Case Study publication *Twitterspace and Facecloud: Social Media for School Librarians* edited by Marianne Bradnock – 12 case studies of UK librarians using Web 2.0 tools in their libraries.

Look too at the Information Landscape section of Joyce Valenza's *Manifesto for the 21st Century School Librarian*[76] that is visionary and thought provoking.

We owe it to our students to give them the range of skills and access to the variety of resources needed to be information literate not only for success within school and the examination system, but for the wider world of home, hobbies and hopefully work.

Remind yourself of your important role in school:

> *People who are more literate are happier, are more likely to be in lasting relationship and living in their own home. Literate people also tend to better paid and smoke less.*
>
> —*Daily Telegraph*, 11 September 2008.

Effective literacy and its key component information literacy, is the gateway to lifelong learning and independent learning. These skills help the learner to develop personal confidence, exam success and increased attainment levels and raise their aspiration too. Information literacy and school libraries are on the cusp of great change – now is the time to give these skills serious focus, time and your energy by

- Reading about them

- Reflecting on them

---

[75] Available at http://www.terry-freedman.org.uk/
web2_2010/Amazing%20Web%202%202%20online%20version.pdf

[76] http://informationfluency.wikispaces.com/
You+know+you%27re+a+21st+century+librarian+if+.+.+.

- Attending training courses about them

- Practising them and modelling them yourself

- Talking and working with your senior leadership team, and with colleagues of all persuasions and subject disciplines across the school to produce coherent and comprehensive information literacy programmes for your students.

Although written nearly a decade ago now this quote is just as relevant today as we work to develop IL in schools:

Challenge for the Future

The greatest challenge facing us today is how to organize information into structured knowledge. We must rise above the obsession with quantity of information and the speed of transmission, and focus on the fact that the key issue for us is our ability to organize the information once it has been amassed, to assimilate it. To find meaning in it, and to assure its survival. And that cannot be done without reading and literacy.

—Dr. Vartan Gregorian, President of the Carnegie Corporation of New York, Keynote Address at the White House conference on school libraries, 2002. http://infolit.org/about-the-national-forum/our-mission/

Giving every child an equal share in the inheritance of achievement which great minds have passed on to us is a great progressive cause... because it is only through learning, the acquisition of intellectual capital – that individuals have the power to shape their own lives.

—Michael Gove, Secretary of State for Education, England. 16 June 2011.

In order to achieve this equal share in the inheritance of achievement that Michael Gove spoke about, we need to re-imagine school libraries fit for the 21st century and we need enthusiastic and visionary school librarians working in partnership with senior leadership teams and teaching and support colleagues to deliver effective information literacy programmes to all their students.

Case Study 1

Chris Shercliff

Librarian/English teacher,
Fair Oak Academy,
Rugeley, Staffordshire

Information Literacy
at Fair Oak Academy

Background

Fair Oak Academy (formerly Fair Oak Business and Enterprise College) is situated in Rugeley, a former mining town on the edge of Cannock Chase in Staffordshire. The Academy site houses students from 11 to 16. Older students attend the Sixth Form Academy in the town centre which is shared with Hagley Park Academy.

The library is brilliantly managed on a day to day basis by Roxanne Blanton, an English graduate with public library experience and line-managed by myself, a Chartered Librarian and former Schools Library Advisor turned English teacher. Following a visit to Werneth School in Stockport in 2008, during which Nikki Heath generously shared her expertise and resources, it was decided to re-write the scheme of work for Information and Library Skills taught to Year 7. Using many of Nikki's ideas we set out a programme of study for fortnightly lessons during which students would learn how to use the library for research and reading for pleasure.

Rationale

However, we had no real model for information literacy used across the College and I was looking for something that I felt our students could relate to. I had seen Helen Emery's BE ALERT model at King Edwards in Lichfield and looked at many other published models but was keen to devise my own for Fair Oak. As an English teacher I knew how much an impact the use of **PEE** (make a **P**oint, give **E**vidence, then **E**xplain) had had on our students' ability to write about a text – the acronym PEE being something that entertained them and helped them to remember the stages. I was hoping to invent something along those lines. After a lot of wrangling with slightly risqué acronyms I eventually, during the summer of 2008, came up with the idea of **KISSING**.

KISSING stands for:

Know what you've got to do

Identify sources of information

Search for relevant information

Select by skimming and scanning

Ignore anything you're not sure about

Now make notes

Give acknowledgement to your sources.

Before I went ahead with the launch of KISSING I ran it past a few colleagues who gave very positive feedback, including our subject leader for ICT who liked it, and subsequently fine-tuned a Year 7 ICT Unit called Using Information and Data Sources so that both units of work complemented each other. I then came up with a poster design and the slogan 'KISSING your work makes it better!' See Appendix 5 (p84).

We introduced the new Unit to Year 7 in September 2008 but I was also able to introduce the KISSING strategy to Year 8 and 9 during SPACE (Social, Personal and Citizenship Education) lessons after negotiating with the relevant Heads of Year. In all cases the students were taken through the strategy stage by stage with the aid of a PowerPoint presentation. They then used the strategy to research a topic of their own choice to present to the rest of their class.

Throughout this time, I was encouraged by both the enthusiasm for the strategy from many teaching colleagues, who agreed that it would be a useful model for research and for presenting findings across subject areas, and also by the support and enthusiasm of the Head Teacher. I was, however, frustrated at being unable to introduce the model to the entire staff, owing to the fact that themes for whole staff meetings were planned so far in advance. Finally, in early 2010, all teachers were given an introduction to the importance of Information Literacy, an overview of the KISSING model and a poster to put in their teaching rooms.

My experience as a teacher, where exam results are paramount, told me that if you can prove that something will improve exam results, teachers are more likely to give it a chance in the classroom, so have plenty of statistics and quotes to support the point you are trying to make (PEEing in action!).

I was also really encouraged to press on with the idea by other Staffordshire schools' library staff at both a local SLA meeting and at a SLA course run by Geoff Dubber.

Current situation

One of the first teachers I showed the model to was our head of ICT, Sue Ramm. She gave me some valuable advice about the format of the KISSING booklet I was working on, and then proceeded to rewrite a scheme of work for Year 7 ICT – Using Information and Data Sources – so that the two units could run alongside each other.

In this unit the students learn to:

- describe some of the different forms that information can come in

- navigate a large website to find specific information

- identify what information is needed for a specific purpose

- identify good question techniques for carrying out surveys

- use search techniques to help me to find specific information on the Internet

- recognise that some websites may be biased and unreliable and ways in which they can identify them.

All of this fits in really well with both our Library and Information Skills Unit and the KISSING strategy. They search websites, carry out internet searches, and explore a multimedia encyclopaedia (Encarta).

The computer room next to the library (accessed by a pair of double doors which fold right back so that it becomes one large space) was originally under the jurisdiction of the ICT department, but this has now been passed on to us so that Roxanne has control over the booking of this room and can use it whenever a teacher brings a class into the library. This means that students can use both books and computers for research. Roxanne is very good at promoting the library to all subject areas and, since her return from maternity leave in May 2010, use of the library/computer room has steadily increased.

Moving forward

Since September 2011, when the college became an Academy, our subject departments have merged with their counterparts from the other Academy in Rugeley, Hagley Park, to form large faculties which work together across both Academies. We have recently been approached by the Director of the English and MFL Faculty, who has asked if Year 7 students from Hagley Park can come to our school library on a fortnightly rota basis to follow our Library and Information Unit and be trained in the KISSING strategy by Roxanne.

Conclusion

On reading through what I have written, what really strikes me is the length of time it has taken us to get this point. This has undoubtedly been because of the increasing demands placed on secondary school staff, meaning that priorities change and some things, like the school library, often seem to end up at the bottom of the list. Having spent many years in a job where school libraries were the most important thing in my life, I can appreciate, for example, how frustrating it must be for the lone practitioner, with no real 'clout' in school, to get things done. I can only reiterate the importance of making sure that, if you want to introduce something which you feel sure will have benefits for everyone, you must make sure that you marshall your evidence in advance and get the backing of the leadership team. The main things to do when trying to achieve this are:

- show how the innovation fits in with the priorities of the school development plan

- gather evidence to show that your idea will increase literacy levels in school

- gather evidence to show that your idea can help to improve exam results.

Resources

Chris Shercliff also shares the following that are available in the Learning and Teaching section of the SLA website at http://www.sla.org.uk/learning-and-teaching.php:

- KISSING conceptual framework poster (also reproduced in Appendix 5, p84)

- A student project planner booklet that uses her KISSING framework

- A 14-slide PowerPoint presentation that she used with students who were working on a Castles factfile for their History homework

- A 32-slide PowerPoint presentation that she used with her teaching colleagues – 'Introducing a Concept Framework for Information Literacy'.

Case Study 2

Lynne Varley, Dip RSA, MCLIP

Librarian, Sponne School, Towcester; SLA School Librarian of the Year Honour List 2009

Information Skills
at Sponne School, Towcester

Background

Sponne School is an academy for 11–18 year olds. It is situated in the market town of Towcester, Northamptonshire, where half the students live in the town and half are bussed in from the villages. There are approximately 1200 students. Last year, our students gained the highest set of GCSE results the school has ever seen, including the critical 5A*–C. Overall, our 5A*–C increased to 88% (up 10% on the previous year) and the 5A*–C including English and Mathematics made a stunning 80% (up 20%). This has placed our school in the top three schools in Northamptonshire. Our A level results continue to be very high. These results have put Sponne in the top three best schools in Northamptonshire.

I have worked at Sponne for nearly fifteen years. In that time, the senior leadership team have provided half the funding to enable me to take my NVQ Level 4 (one of the few!) on Information and Library Services. I was included and successfully completed the staff training for the IT Learning Schools Programme in 2003. In 2006/7, Sponne Library was selected as Best Secondary School Library of Northamptonshire by the Northamptonshire schools' library service. In 2008/9, I was invited to be a judge. We participated again in 2010/11 and were runners up. I was supported by Sponne and achieved my chartership in 2007 and reached the Honours List of School Librarian of the Year in 2009.

The Library at Sponne

When I started at Sponne, the library had nine computers with just one with access to the internet and it was so slow that I could have gone and made a cup of tea while it was connecting! I kid you not! A bit different to the current situation of 17 computers in our Learning Resource Centre (LRC), all connected to the internet with a fairly fast connection and access to a further 15 at break and lunch time in an adjoining room.

Information skills have always been an important part of a school library in my opinion and in my time at Sponne, I have gradually approached departments to see what we could do to improve information literacy in students. I feel it is important to expose students to different types of resources and the LRC is a vital area where students can experience these in information skills lessons. I understand that some Head Teachers are disposing of their school libraries and replacing them with IT suites. In my opinion this is a retrograde step. I am naturally in favour of the use of computers for research but I still feel that to have an area (read library) that houses a fiction and non-fiction collection, magazines, newspapers, career literature, story CDs and film DVDs, as well as computers gives students a well rounded provision of resources. I find it disappointing that neither the Labour nor the Coalition Governments would commit to making school libraries statutory, a cause fronted by children's author Alan Gibbons (http://www.alangibbons.com).

The situation still leaves the decision to the Head Teachers as to whether they should retain a school library. The Sponne School management is committed to the importance of a broad-based LRC and this has been a critical factor in the development of our literacy and information literacy initiatives.

Why is a school library relevant to the curriculum?

It is very important to give students as wide a variety of fiction as possible to cater for differing reading levels and tastes. It is vital to interest those who are struggling to read and to fuel those who love reading with a selection of modern and classic novels. The LRC is the best place as it also has the staff with the knowledge and enthusiasm to encourage and recommend authors and titles, coupled with the opportunity to build a picture of students' individual needs and tastes.

Apart from the fiction, however, it is vital for students to be exposed to magazines, newspapers and non-fiction books as well as online paid resources. The internet has a mass of useful information but also the opposite. If young people find it difficult to disseminate information from a book which has been written specifically for their age range and possibly differentiated for those with special needs, how much more difficult is it to surf the internet and find credible and accessible information? Learning how to assess the validity of a site is a skill that even adults find difficult.

Introducing Information Literacy

Until about six years ago I had introduced:

- An LRC Induction for Year 7s and new staff
- An information skills package for Year 7s in Geography on the local area – students had to answer questions using books and pamphlets on the local area, local maps (both street and ordnance survey) and websites

- An information skills package for Year 8s on Shakespeare – I adapted question sheets on Shakespeare's life, the theatre in Tudor times, Shakespeare's plays and Tudor times with extension questions such as 'A day in the life of a Tudor actor' from a resource called 'Search and Discover' by Claire Drury and students found the answers using both books and the internet

- An information skills package for Year 9s on the Home Front in World War II.

Case study

World War II: Home Front

I was fortunate to have the opportunity to produce a resource which introduced the topic of World War II (Home Front) to our Year 9s. Together with a fellow school librarian, Hilary Sutton of Bishop Stopford School and Sue Polchow, (then a Senior Advisor and IT specialist for the service) who provided the IT expertise and advice, we took advantage of a Northamptonshire Council scheme offering funding to schools to release staff time for the development of a curriculum project.

Initially, Hilary and I discussed the project with our respective Heads of History to decide on a mutually agreed topic. Throughout the construction we continually referred to them to ensure that the end product would be of use.

Our goal was to produce a video introduction to project researching using an actual Year 9 student, which would be used at Sponne and Bishop Stopford Schools and could be networked across the East Midlands Broadband consortium schools network portal. We used a product called Boxmind, which is no longer in existence, but which was then a recent acquisition, by Sponne School.

Boxmind utilised a combination of video, PowerPoint and Microsoft Word on the same screen. A video of a student researching the Home Front in the library was shot by me with a voiceover giving advice on how to find resources using the computer catalogue (OPAC), note taking, the correct use of copying and pasting, referencing etc. The video was backed up by PowerPoint slides showing the student's questions giving simple research advice and support. Clicking on points on slides linked through to further slides with additional subject information, resource links and research advice. A word document was scrolling along the bottom of the screen with the script from the voiceover.

The actual videoing and script took us a day to put together. Through liaison with the Sponne drama department, a suitable student actor was recruited. This was my first attempt with a video camera, having only practiced once the day before and I swiftly decided to use shots of the student concerned when he wasn't moving! The voice over was my colleague Hilary who sounded very professional. We produced the PowerPoint slides over a three month period and this required research at our main public library in Northampton to provide photographs from the period and permissions from publishers to allow pictures of the books we suggested. Further support was given by my line manager who was an expert at cutting and splicing video. In the end, the software could not be made to run smoothly on the East Midlands portal and the final product had to be run from a CD on Sponne School's own system which eventually was placed on the school server for easier access.

Year 9 students came to the LRC for the first lesson of their project. The six minute video was used to introduce the concept of researching and then students used the LRC to pursue their research. Feedback showed that students enjoyed this 'shadowing' method of introduction. However, the difficulties with the Boxmind software meant that online links could not be updated, and to style-sensitive teenagers the student actor now seems old fashioned, so the product is no longer used. I have learnt from this experience to ensure that suppliers are realistic and accurate about the capabilities of their product. It was very time-consuming and we spent a fair amount of our own time to complete the package. We were the first department in the school to utilise this product and it is important to keep aware of developments within the school into which the LRC might tap. I am currently considering the potential of Sponne School's recent move to the Frog VLE.

Case study **Study Skills sessions for Sixth Form Geography**

I approached teachers of sixth form students about information skills lessons tailored to their requirements and the Head of Geography took me up on the opportunity. The students were just starting coursework on a number of different essay assignments of which the teacher had advised me, so I provided a PowerPoint introduction, to demonstrate the use of our OPAC, the range of online resources that we subscribed to that I deemed relevant, advice on advanced searching on the internet, alternative search and meta search engines, warnings regarding validity of sites compared with printed resources and last but not least plagiarism. I talked about the resources we hold in the LRC and supported the talk with help sheets that included hints on advanced searching and a list of useful resources including websites. This was followed by research in the LRC using both our printed and computer resources.

Developing Information Literacy in the curriculum

I felt I was scratching the surface of information literacy at Sponne and then about six years ago a number of circumstances coincided to focus my thoughts. A course by Geoff Dubber on 'Information Literacy Skills', a visit to Luton University library (now the University of Bedford) and the introduction to our Acting Head of English, Jo Holliday, later to become our Literacy Co-ordinator.

The course by Geoff Dubber encouraged me to consider producing a whole school Information Literacy Policy. I sought advice from the Northamptonshire Schools' Library Service and also the Acting Head of English who provided me with the necessary documents to support my policy. With the latter's assistance, we presented my policy proposals to the Senior Leadership Team, who then invited us to talk to the whole school staff at an INSET – scary!

Presenting to the teaching and support staff was the crucial turning point in the school's approach to information literacy. The staff was very enthusiastic and keen to take up the opportunities offered by the LRC. The policy was then accepted by the governing body.

Shortly after this, our Science Department contacted me regarding their GCSE course and the 'controlled assessment' coursework element which had been introduced recently. Year 10 students were given a question which changed each year. This one was 'Should we spend time in the sun?' Students had an opportunity to research this question and bring the results of their research into the classroom where they would answer the question in exam conditions using the evidence to back up their arguments for or against. They were able to gain higher marks by using a range of resources to present their argument and therefore enhancing students' ability to access these was imperative e.g. newspaper articles, books, websites. We ran lessons in the LRC for the Science classes demonstrating the types of resources available for them to use.

By this time, with the encouragement of our Acting Head of English, we had introduced fortnightly library lessons within the English timetable using a booklet she had used at another school. This has since been adapted a number of times to suit Sponne students. Following our INSET, we introduced five information skills lessons for Year 8 on different subjects, in consultation with the departments concerned. These were:

- Caribbean and Latin American Music
- History of Transport from 1750 – 1900
- Weather Hazards

- An introduction to Shakespeare
- Space Junk.

Throughout these lessons we emphasised the use of the non-fiction resources, the online resources and the internet. We reminded students how to use the OPAC, talked about correct note taking and provided a reference sheet for each of the subjects for use by the students to encourage the habit of keeping a bibliography of their research. This has already paid dividends as teachers are finding that students are beginning to do this as a matter of course.

In the last few years, we have run Careers lessons to Year 8 students before they choose their options, our school having adopted a two year Key Stage Three. The lessons in the LRC focus on the paper resources available and we model this with a job wheel, followed by the students researching a particular job and filling in their own job wheel – job content, personal qualities, qualifications, pay, training, prospects etc.

However, this shift in Key Stage structure has also placed pressure on Year 8 teaching and some of the departments have pulled out of the Year 8 LRC sessions as they do not have time to include them in their timetable, though other opportunities have arisen with Year 7 and 9.

With the Coalition Government's plans for further revision of the curriculum, it is important to acknowledge that we have to be flexible and adjust to the pressures and opportunities within the school's teaching experience. It also means that LRC staff has to work continuously at maintaining a good working relationship with teachers.

Information Literacy and Plagiarism

During my preparation for chartership I was required to have knowledge of different types of libraries. I approached a friend who is a librarian at the University of Bedford, Jo Myhill, Head of Academic Liaison, and she kindly agreed to show me their library. At that time Jo was active in delivering information skills to new students and she was and is passionate about plagiarism. She explained that like many universities, plagiarism was a problem. The ease with which students could: cut and paste from the internet and the lack of understanding on referencing techniques and note-taking skills are the major causes of plagiarism offences. Currently, Learning Resources at Bedford are in discussions with the university on the issues of dealing with low level plagiarism and how the library and study skills staff can help students overcome the problem. In 2007 she presented a paper at a LILAC (Librarians' Information Literacy Annual Conference) conference. I returned to school with the intention that if possible our students would not be ignorant of the issues of plagiarism.

Jo very kindly agreed to talk to Year 12 students about these issues bringing an awareness of what is expected at university and stressing how important it is to start developing the appropriate information skills at school. These have been followed up by my information skills lessons to Sixth Form, which include warnings about the problem. These lessons since the INSET have multiplied and in the last two years I have run lessons for students of PE, Media Studies, History, Geography, Business Studies, Psychology, Sociology and Law.

Case study

PE citation game

I was asked by the PE department to do a similar introduction for their students. These students are often not very academic and are not regular library users; indeed some have only used the LRC in the past as part of a formal class. As a starter to the lesson, I placed a selection of books and magazines relating to PE on a number of tables along with slips of paper. The slips each contained a single element of the information needed to construct a Harvard citation reference, such as publisher or title or author. I then challenged them to find and match up all the necessary elements with the appropriate resource. I found that this proved a more memorable way of them becoming acquainted with the necessity of referencing than a talk on the subject. This was then built on with further introduction to carrying out research as I had done with the Geography lesson but tailored to their requirements.

Where are we now?

Information Literacy at Sponne is becoming a whole school objective. My policy was a starting point and it continues to evolve. It is important to ensure that we are all reiterating the same principles of practice. Reflecting on my journey with information skills I have concluded that:

- It is important to have the commitment and understanding of the Head Teacher and senior management. I am fortunate that Sponne School has both a fully supportive staff and senior leadership team. I think it is an essential factor that I am now included in the Faculty Leadership team since this has given me status within the school.

- In my experience I have found that I need to be proactive and approach departments. The subject departments are too busy to think of library resources without the occasional nudge. Attending faculty meetings has given me the opportunity to find out curriculum changes and be ready to approach teachers with suggestions for activities.

■ Information Literacy needs to be relevant. We need to be able to demonstrate how these skills deliver results for students in curriculum activities.

■ Advocacy is essential. Librarians need to put themselves forward through INSET, through involvement in school planning and by networking with supportive staff. It is important to communicate what the LRC is doing and to report to management. I have a fortnightly meeting with my line manager who is an Assistant Head Teacher.

■ I have experienced a number of setbacks on the journey. Establishing Information Literacy as a whole school focus has taken years to nurture and it is still a challenge to maintain the momentum.

Bibliography

Drury, Claire (2000). *Search and Discover*. Carel Press, Carlisle.

Dubber, Geoff (2005). SLA Guidelines Plus: *Information Matters: Developing Information Skills through the Secondary School LRC*. School Library Association, Swindon.

Gibbons, Alan (2009) Petition to the Government to make school libraries statutory. http://www.number10.gov.uk/Page22227

Myhill, Jo (Head of Academic Liaison, Bedford University) (2007)

LILAC 2007 Posters and Parallel Sessions available at http://www.lilacconference.com/dw/archive/2007/posters.html (accessed 3 February 2010)

School Library Association http://www.sla.org.uk

Sponne School Technological College available at http://www.sponneschool.northants.sch.uk/ (accessed 3 February 2010)

Further Reading

Books

Barwood, Tom (2005). *Learning to Learn Pocketbook* (2005). Teachers' Pocketbooks.

Buzan, Tony (2006). *The Buzan Study Skills Handbook*. BBC Active.

Carver, Kirsty; Fisher, Karen; Park, Alison (eds) (2008). *The Little Book of Information Skills*. Libraries and Learning Innovation. Leeds Metropolitan University. http://skillsforlearning.leedsmet.ac.uk/publications.shtml Accessed 16 Mar. 2012.

Cottrell. Stella (2011). *Critical Thinking Skills*. Palgrave Macmillan.

Cottrell, Stella (2008). *The Study Skills Handbook*. Palgrave Macmillan.

De Bono, Edward (2008). *Six Frames for Thinking About Information*. Vermilion.

Dolowitz, David; Buckler, Steve; Sweeney, Fionnghuala (2008). *Researching Online*. Palgrave.

Drury, Claire (2000). *Search and Discover*. Carel Press.

Dubber, Geoff (2008). *A Primary School Information Skills Toolkit*. School Library Association. 978-1-903446-44-7

Dubber, Geoff (2008). *Cultivating Curiosity: Information Literacy Skills and th Primary School Library*. School Library Association. 978-1-903446-42-3

Freedman, Terry (ed). *The Amazing Web 2.0 Projects Book*
Tried and tested ideas for using Web 2.0 in education. A freeload (120+ pages) at http://www.ictineducation.org/free-stuff/ Accessed 13 Oct. 2011.

Godrey, Jeanne (2010). *Reading and Making Notes: Pocket Study Skills*. Palgrave Macmillan.

Godwin, Janet (2009). *Planning Your Essay: Pocket Study Skills*. Palgrave Macmillan.

Godwin, Peter and Parker, Jo (2008). *Information Literacy Meets Library 2.0* Facet Publishing.

Grey, Duncan (2006). *Getting the Buggers to Learn*. Continuum.

Grey, Duncan (2006). *Implementing an Information Literacy Programme For Your School*. Tribal.
http://www.sfe.co.uk/products/product-details.cfm?id=121
Accessed 18 Oct. 2011. (This is a staff development folder and disk.)

Holtom, Elizabeth (2007). *Study Skills: The Complete Guide To Smart Learning*. Galore Park.

James, Mary (2009). *AQA Extended Project Student Companion*. Nelson Thornes.

Konstant, Tim and Taylor, Morris (2008). *Overcoming Information Overload*. Hodder Education.

Kuhlthau, Carol; Maniotes, Leslie; Caspari, Ann (2007). *Inquiry Learning in the 21st Century*. Libraries Unlimited.

Mackey, Thomas P. and Jacobson, Trudi E. (eds). *Collaborative Information Literacy Assessments: Strategies for Evaluating Teaching and Learning*. Facet. 978-1-85604-706-7

Pears, Richard and Shields, Graham (2010). *Cite Them Right. The Essential Referencing Guide*. Palgrave Macmillan. (A book for Higher Education but with some interesting ideas for schools.)

Pulman, Andy (2009). *Blogs, Wikis, Podcasts and More: Pocket Study Skills*. Palgrave Macmillan.

Richardson, L. and McBryde-Wilding, H. (2009). *Information Skills for Education Students*. Learning Matters.

Solomon, Amy; Wilson, Gwyn; Taylor, Terry (2012). 2nd ed. *100% Information Literacy Success*. Wadsworth Cengage Learning.

Williams, Kate and Carroll, Jude (2009). *Referencing and Understanding Plagiarism: Pocket Study Skills*. Palgrave Macmillan.

Articles/Reports

Brockman, John. How Is the Internet Changing Our Brains? http://www.edge.org/q2010/q10_index.html Accessed 13 Oct. 2011.

Dase, Annike. Information Literacy and our Primary School Library, *The School Librarian* vo.59. no3 autumn 2011 (although written with a primary school perspective this is an article well worth reading)

Head, Alison and Eisenberg, Michael (Dec 2010) How College Students Seek Information in the Digital Age http://projectinfolit.org/pdfs/PIL_Fall2009_Year1Report_12_2009.pdf Accessed 13 Oct. 2011.

Head, Alison and Eisenberg, Michael (July 2010) How Handouts for Research Assignments Guide Today's College Students http://projectinfolit.org/pdfs/PIL_Handout_Study_finalvJuly_2010.pdf Accessed 14 Oct. 2011.

Herring, Mark Y. 10 Reasons Why the Internet Is No Substitute for a Library. http://www.ala.org/ala/alonline/resources/slctdarticles/10reasonswhy.cfm Accessed 13 Oct. 2011.

Mittermeyer, Diane and Quirion, Diane. (2003) Information Literacy: Study of Incoming First-Year Undergraduates in Quebec. http://www.crepuq.qc.ca/documents/bibl/formation/studies_Ang.pdf Accessed 14 Oct. 2011.

Williams, Dorothy and Wavell, Caroline. (2006) Information Literacy in the Classroom: Secondary School Teachers' Conceptions. Robert Gordon University. http://www4.rgu.ac.uk/files/acf4daa.pdf Accessed 18 Oct. 2011.

Williams, Dorothy and Wavell, Caroline.(2006) Untangling Spaghetti? The Complexity of Developing Information Literacy in Secondary School Students. Robert Gordon University. http://www.scotland.gov.uk/Resource/Doc/924/0093122.pdf Accessed 18 Oct. 2011.

Websites

You Tube. Slideshare. Do have a look at both these sites – there is a whole range of material under familiar search terms. For example:

Plagiarism
http://www.youtube.com/watch?v=Mwbw9KF-ACYandsns=em
This is in Norwegian with English subtitles, but still worth a look.
Accessed 14 Oct. 2011

Librarians Do Gaga: Information Retrieval from the University of Washington Information School http://www.youtube.com/watch?v=a_uzUh1VT98
Accessed 14 Oct. 2011.

Dewey Numbers.
http://www.deweydigger.com/ Accessed 14 Oct. 2011.

Information Literacy.
http://www.informationliteracy.org.uk/ Accessed 14 Oct. 2011.
This website has been designed and developed by information professionals from key UK organisations actively involved in the field of information literacy. The site supports practitioners by providing news, case studies, examples of best practice and freely available tool kits. Our aim is to provide a practical resource that information professionals regularly visit to discover the latest developments in information literacy.

Daanen, Hans. Facer, Keri (2007) 2020 and Beyond FutureLab http://www2.futurelab.org.uk/resources/publications-reports-articles/opening education-reports/Opening-Education-Report663

Internet Detective. A free Internet tutorial
www.vtstutorials.ac.uk/detective/ Accessed 13 Oct. 2011.

California Polytechnic State University – a useful site for general study skills ideas – including an interesting section on procrastination!
http://www.sas.calpoly.edu/asc/ssl.html Accessed 13 Oct. 2011.

Cardiff University Information Services. *Handbook for Information Literacy Teaching* (2009 updated to 2011) All 208 pages. An absolutely brilliant and comprehensive handbook for HE produced by Nigel Morgan and his team, but all the basics there for school librarians.
http://www.cardiff.ac.uk/insrv/educationandtraining/infolit/hilt/
Accessed 13 Oct. 2011.

Itscotland is a well known site for Scottish schools – some excellent information literacy materials for all ages
http://www.ltscotland.org.uk/studyskills/index.asp
Accessed 13 Oct. 2011.

La Trobe University, Melbourne, Australia – a useful IL framework that could be adapted for school use
http://www.latrobe.edu.au/policy/documents/information-literacy-procedure.pdf (See pages 4 and 5)
http://latrobe.libguides.com/libskills.
Accessed 13 Oct. 2011. These Teach Yourself Library skills pages may give you ideas for what you can do yourself in your school

National Forum Information Literacy
http://infolit.org/about-the-national-forum/welcome/
Based in Cambridge, Massachusetts, USA, this is an important reference point for those interested in US information literacy

NHS Education for Scotland. – Although targeted to NHS professionals you will find some excellent Information Literacy material that gives simple explanations to the various stages in the research cycle
http://www.infoliteracy.scot.nhs.uk/home.aspx

Open University – some excellent material here, essentially for HE but potential material for Sixth Formers.
http://www.open.ac.uk/infoskills-researchers/information-introduction.htm
Accessed 13 Oct. 2011.

Transitioning to College. Tips for first year university students
http://www.transitioning2college.org/
Accessed 14 Oct. 2011.

University of Salford. Reading and notemaking. Staff and Curriculum Development
http://www.careers.salford.ac.uk/cms/resources/uploads/File/staff2.pdf
Accessed 18 Oct. 2011.

University of Sheffield – Information Skills Resource. Some useful quizzes
http://www.librarydevelopment.group.shef.ac.uk/showcase.html
Accessed 13 Oct. 2011.

Welsh Information Literacy Project – some very good material here including some case studies that feature two secondary schools. *Information Literacy Framework for Wales: Finding and using information in 21st century Wales.* Cardiff University, 2011. http://librarywales.org/uploads/media/Information_Literacy_Framework_Wales.pdf
Accessed 1 Mar. 2012.

Appendix 1: Research Sequences

Marland 9 Step Sequence	The Big6™	The PLUS Model	The key teaching skills to develop through curriculum-based IL programmes	Essential sub-skills to be taught. Practising and developed through secondary schooling.
What Do I Need to Do?	Task definition	Purpose	Planning	Activating prior knowledge Asking Questions Fixing parameters to a possible study Time management Planning a task sequence – small steps Gathering appropriate equipment Organising the learning environment Considering marking criteria Examination revision planning
Where Could I Go? How Do I Get the Information?	Information Seeking Strategies	Location	Locating and Gathering	Identifying possible/probable information sources – libraries, museums, archives, photo libraries, people Considering useful keywords Using search engines effectively Using on-line databases Using Dewey effectively Searching newspapers and journals Being aware of e-safety issues Identifying relevant websites Identifying appropriate levels of information Identifying the author authority Using the phone to gather information Using email and Web.2.0 Surmising when you have enough resources to start the enquiry

Question		Process	Skills
Which Resources Shall I Use?		Selecting and Appraising	Skimming and scanning; Understanding copyright issues; Recognising bias. Currency. Inaccuracy
How Shall I Use the Resources?	Use of Information	Use	
What Shall I Make a Record Of?		Organising and Recording	Use of copy and paste; Plagiarism and Referencing/Citation; Using footnotes; Note making techniques – use of post-it notes, 'card-sort'; Using highlighters in various ways; Use of photocopier, digital camera, camcorder, scanner; Using txt messaging
Have I Got the Information I Need?			
How Should I Present It?	Synthesis	Communicating and Realising	Using a range of software; Essay writing; Using a spell checker; Adding a contents page, indexes, glossary, further reading/bibliography; Editing; Proof reading; Peer reviewing
What Have I Achieved?	Evaluation / Self-evaluation and Sources	Evaluating	Reflecting on working methods used; Accepting constructive peer and adult criticisms

Appendix 2: Answers to questions in Table 2

Table 2.

ILS Activity: Demonstrating the Importance of ILS within the KS3 learning objectives for English and ICT.

Creating an ILS progressive school programme.

ENGLISH

Strand 5: Reading for meaning:understanding and responding to print, electronic and multi-modal texts

    5.1 Developing and adapting active reading skills and strategies.

ICT

Strand 1: Finding Information

    1.1 Using data and information sources

National Curriculum learning objective	Year	Subject
Make relevant notes when gathering ideas from texts	7	English
Select information for a task from a range of sources and be aware of the relative strengths and weaknesses of these sources	7	ICT
Make relevant notes when researching different sources, comparing and contrasting information	8	English
Use a range of reading strategies to retrieve relevant information and main points from a text distinguishing between fact and opinion where appropriate	8	English
Justify the use of particular information sources to support an investigation or presentation and devise and apply criteria to evaluate how well various information types support a task	8	ICT
Recognise how the content and style of information can influence the message it gives and that data can be distorted or misused	8	ICT
Acknowledge all sources, recognising copyright and other constraints	8	ICT
Select from a range of strategies the most appropriate ways to locate, retrieve and compare information and ideas from a variety of texts	9	English
Make relevant notes in a range of formats and approaches when researching a variety of sources	9	English
Collect data systematically from sources for an identified purpose	9	ICT

Criteria	Level	Average Age
Pupils read a range of texts fluently and accurately. They read independently, using strategies appropriately to establish meaning. In responding to fiction and non-fiction they show understanding of the main points and express preferences. **They use their knowledge of the alphabet to locate books and find information.**	3	Y4/5 Age 8/9
In responding to a range of texts, pupils show understanding of significant ideas, themes, events and characters, beginning to use inference and deduction. They understand that texts reflect the time and culture in which they were written. **They refer to the text when explaining their views and are able to locate and use ideas and information.**	4	Y6/7 Age 10/11
Pupils show understanding of a range of texts, selecting essential points and using inference and deduction where appropriate. In their responses, they identify key features, themes and characters and select sentences, phrases and relevant information to support their views. They understand that texts fit into historical and literary traditions. **They retrieve and collate information from a range of sources.**	5	Y7/8 Age 12/13
In reading and discussing a range of texts, pupils identify different layers of meaning and comment on their significance and effect. They give personal responses to literary texts, referring to aspects of language, structure and themes in justifying their views, and making connections between texts from different times and cultures and their own experiences. **They summarise a range of information from different sources.**	6	Y8/9 Age 13/14
Pupils show understanding of the ways in which meaning and information are conveyed in a range of texts. They articulate personal and critical responses to poems, plays and novels, showing awareness of their thematic, structural and linguistic features. **They understand why some texts are particularly valued and influential. They select, synthesise and compare information from a variety of sources.**	7	14+ GCSE
Pupils' responses show their appreciation of, and **ability to comment on a range of texts**, and they evaluate how authors achieve their effects through the use of linguistic, structural and presentational devices. **They select and analyse information and ideas, and comment on how these are conveyed in different texts.** They explore some of the ways in which texts from different times and cultures have influenced literature and society.	8	14+ GCSE A-C

Appendix 4: A sample of appropriate freeware tools

IL Key Target Skill	Freeware tool example
Planning	**Get organised** **Toodledo** http://www.toodledo.com Get organized with a to-do list – also available for the iPhone **Generate ideas** **WiseMapping** http://www.wisemapping.com Generate and organize your ideas in visual formats **Mindmeister** www.mindmeister.com **Edraw Mind Map** http://www.edrawsoft.com/freemind.php **Free Mind** http://freemind.sourceforge.net/wiki/index.php/Main_Page **Revision Planner** **BBC Revision Planners** http://www.bbc.co.uk/schools/studentlife/ revisionandskills/revision/revision_planners.shtml
Locating & Gathering	**Bookmark web sites** **Delicious** http://delicious.com Store, organize and share all your bookmarks **Organize your stuff online** **Netvibes** http://www.netvibes.com Create a personalized homepage and add widgets to organize your stuff online **Collaborate with others** **Voicethread** http://voicethread.com "Group conversations around images, documents and videos" **Carry out a survey** **SurveyMonkey** http://www.surveymonkey.com Design a survey, collect responses and analyse your results

	Read news feeds (RSS) **Google Reader** http://www.google.com/reader/view/#overview-page **Contact colleagues to discuss the project** **Twitter** http://twitter.com/ **Create your own blog or website to gather information** **Wordpress** http://wordpress.org/ **Email alerts** **Google Alerts** http://www.google.com/alerts **Video conferencing** **Oovoo** http://www.oovoo.com/
Selecting & Appraising	**Look up words and their meanings** **Visuwords** http://www.visuwords.com Word meanings and their associations in diagram format **Wordnik** http://www.wordnik.com/ "Words and everything about them" Not comprehensive but uses examples and pictures
Organising & Recording	**Memorize facts** **Cramberry** http://cramberry.net **Create flashcards online to help you memorize things** **ProProfs** http://www.proprofs.com/flashcards/ **Put events in a timeline** **TimeGlider** http://timeglider.com See history by creating online, interactive timelines

	Collaborative creating, sharing, storing of information **Google Docs** https://docs.google.com/#home **Flowchart** http://flowchart.com/ **Create your own MP3's** **Audacity** http://audacity.sourceforge.net/
Communicating & Realising	**Collaborate with others** **Voicethread** http://voicethread.com "Group conversations around images, documents and videos" **Add pictures** **Flickr** http://flickrcc.bluemountains.net Millions of photos licensed for use under creative commons Can be used in your own work as long as you credit the creator **Make pictures with words** **Wordle** http://www.wordle.net Make colourful word clouds from text or web pages The more often a word appears, the bigger it looks in the Wordle **Create a poster** **Glogster** http://www.glogster.com Discover the world of glogging and make posters that use sound and video clips **Share PowerPoint presentations** **Slideshare** http://www.slideshare.net Find PowerPoint presentations on subjects that interest you or upload your own **Create a video/animated slide show** **Animoto** http://animoto.com Produces videos using your photos, video clips and music

	Compile a bibliography **EasyBib** http://www.easybib.com **Neil's Toolbox** http://www.neilstoolbox.com/bibliography-creator Reference books the correct way **Create an online booklet** **Issuu** http://issuu.com/ **Create and share** **Scratch** http://scratch.mit.edu/ Create and share your own interactive stories, games, music and art
Evaluating	I can't find anything appropriate for this skill

This list is also available in the Learning and Teaching section of the SLA website at
http://www.sla.org.uk/learning-and-teaching.php

Chris Shercliff: Fair Oak Academy

Know what you've got to do – find and highlight ➝ **keywords**

Identify sources of information

books/magazines   computers

experts

Search for relevant information

Select the bits you want to use by **skimming** and **scanning**

use your eyes!

Ignore stuff you're not sure about – check for bias, honesty and the author's qualifications

Now **make notes!**
• bullet points, lists, mindmaps, spiders,
Re-present in chosen **format** – **BUT**
Don't just copy and paste unless you……

Give acknowledgement to your sources
Make a **bibliography!**

your work makes it better!

84

Natural Disasters Project: Where Do I Start?

When you are doing research on a big topic like Natural Disasters, you need to narrow down what you are going to work on in order to focus your research.

Work through the following activities with the person next to you to help you do this.

Task 1: What do you already know about natural disasters?

I have written one fact about natural disasters below. Write two more things that you already know about natural disasters.

1. Volcanoes erupt when molten lava spews up from under the earth's crust.

2.

3.

Task 2: Now underline the key words in your sentence.

The key words can be turned into questions that you will answer when you do your research. I have used my fact on volcanoes to write the questions below.

Use the facts you wrote down in Task 1 to write questions you could answer during your research. Try to think of a question for each of the question words below.

How is lava formed?

Where do we find volcanoes?

What problems are caused when volcanoes erupt?

What...

Where...

When...

How...

Why...

Choose one or more of your questions to be the focus for your research project.

Also available from the SLA

SLA Survival Guide: Making it Through Your First Few Years as a School Librarian

Edited by Anne-Marie Tarter and Geoff Dubber

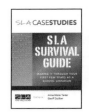

978-1-903446-54-6   £9.00 (non-members £12.00)

The role of school librarian is one of the most exciting, challenging, rewarding and important posts in any school. This excellent addition to our Case Studies series outlines the combined wisdom of one senior SLA officer and School Library Service manager and ten highly skilled and determined school librarians who have all featured in SLA School Librarian of the Year awards. All have wide experience of different areas of teaching and learning and working in school libraries of various sorts and sizes.

All the major aspects of running a library are considered – enjoy it and be inspired by their particular stories and advice.

Crossing the Divide: Induction and Transition in the Secondary School LRC

by Geoff Dubber

978-1-903446-52-2   £9.00 (non-members £12.00)

This popular Guideline Plus is now republished in a fully updated and expanded edition incorporating the latest government thinking across the UK about induction at age 11+ in general and how these thoughts can be applied to school library work.

It also includes transition ideas for the 14+ students about to start exam courses, induction for Sixth Formers and the often neglected area of adults new to the school too. Reference is also made to creating induction links between schools and higher education.

Some new case studies complete this essential title on developing positive attitudes in newcomers and a focused working environment throughout the secondary school.

Cool, Calm and Collected: Managing Behaviour in the Secondary School Library

by Claire Larson and Geoff Dubber

978-1-903446-49-2   £9.00 (non-members £12.00)

Working effectively with young people and adults in a busy secondary school library is an essential part of the work of all the staff. The earlier edition of this popular Guideline had been out of print for three years, but the book has now been fully updated and revised in the light of 'Every Child Matters'.

With a range of new case studies written by established and well known school librarians who share their own experiences, it will look at the issues surrounding behaviour management – style and image, body language, use of whole school policies and of course it suggests strategies to use with groups and individuals. It also includes a section on working with adults in the school library context – not always the easiest of users.